M. J. Heale	The American R
M. J. Heale	Franklin D. Roosevelt
Ruth Henig	The Origins of the First World War
Ruth Henig	The Origins of the Second World War 1933–1939
Ruth Henig	Versailles and After 1919–1933
P. D. King	Charlemagne
Stephen J. Lee	Peter the Great
Stephen J. Lee	The Thirty Years War
J. M. MacKenzie	The Partition of Africa 1880–1900
John W. Mason	The Cold War 1945–1991
Michael Mullett	Calvin
Michael Mullett	The Counter-Reformation
Michael Mullett	James II and English Politics 1678–1688
Michael Mullett	Luther
D. G. Newcombe	Henry VIII and the English Reformation
Robert Pearce	Attlee's Labour Governments 1945–1951
Gordon Phillips	The Rise of the Labour Party 1893–1931
John Plowright	Regency England
Hans A. Pohlsander	The Emperor Constantine
J. H. Shennan	France before the Revolution
J. H. Shennan	International Relations in Europe 1689–1789
J. H. Shennan	Louis XIV
Margaret Shennan	The Rise of Brandenburg-Prussia
David Shotter	Augustus Caesar
David Shotter	The Fall of the Roman Republic
David Shotter	Tiberius Caesar
Richard Stoneman	Alexander the Great
Keith J. Stringer	The Reign of Stephen
John Thorley	Athenian Democracy
John K. Walton	Disraeli
John K. Walton	The Second Reform Act
Michael J. Winstanley	Gladstone and the Liberal Party
Michael J. Winstanley	Ireland and the Land Question 1800–1922

LANCASTER PAMPHLETS

Hitler and Nazism

Second Edition

Dick Geary

ROUTLEDGE

Taylor & Francis Group

London and New York

First published 2000
by Routledge
11 New Fetter Lane, London EC4P 4EE

Simultaneously published in the USA and Canada
by Routledge
29 West 35th Street, New York, NY 10001

Routledge is an imprint of the Taylor & Francis Group

© 2000 Dick Geary

Typeset in Bembo by BC Typesetting, Bristol
Printed and bound in Great Britain by
Biddles Ltd, Guildford and King's Lynn

British Library Cataloguing in Publication Data
A catalogue record for this book is available from the British Library

Library of Congress Cataloging in Publication Data
Geary, Dick.
Hitler and Nazism/Dick Geary. – 2nd ed.
p.   cm. – (Lancaster pamphlets)
Includes bibliographical references.
1. Hitler, Adolf, 1889–1945.
2. Heads of state–Germany–Biography.
3. Germany–Politics and government–1918–1933.
4. Germany–Politics and government–1933–1945.
5. National socialism.–History.
I. Title. II. Series.
DD247.H5 G33 2000
943.086'092–dc21
[B]   00-027569

ISBN 0–415–20226–4

Contents

Preface to the Second Edition

At the end of January 1933 Adolf Hitler was appointed German Chancellor. Within a few months his National Socialist German Workers' Party (NSDAP) – the Nazis – had suspended civil liberties, destroyed almost all independent economic, social and political organisations and established a one-party state. That state persecuted many of its own citizens, starting with the Nazis' political opponents, the Communists and Social Democrats. Thereafter the gates of the prisons and concentration camps were opened to take in other 'undesirables': delinquents, the 'work-shy', tramps, 'habitual criminals', homosexuals, freemasons, Jehovah's Witnesses and – most notoriously – gypsies and Jews. In 1939 the Third Reich unleashed what became, especially on its Eastern front, a war of almost unparalleled barbarism and slaughter. Furthermore, while some 70,000 of the mentally ill and incurably infirm were murdered in the 'euthanasia' programme, various organisations of state, party and the army embarked upon the attempted extermination of European Jewry in the gas chambers of Auschwitz, Treblinka, Madianek and Sobibor.

With such a record it is scarcely surprising that the rise of Nazism and the policies of the Third Reich have been subjected to massive historical scrutiny. The proliferation of literature before the first edition of this pamphlet had made it almost impossible for even the professional historian to keep track of research and retain an overview. Since 1993 the difficulty has become even greater. This edition, like the first, attempts to analyse key themes (the role of Hitler, the factors that brought him to power, the structure and nature of government in the Third Reich, the relationship between that government and the German people, and the origins and implementation of the Holocaust) in the light of that research. In such a brief survey certain areas will not be discussed, in particular Hitler's foreign policy and the origins of the Second World War (a topic covered in another Lancaster Pamphlet).

Since the appearance of *Hitler and Nazism,* there have been some marked shifts in the emphasis of research. In this new edition, therefore, more space is devoted to the role of women, the restructuring of labour, questions of modernisation and, above all, the centrality of race to all areas of policy between 1933 and 1945. The section on the social bases of Nazi support before 1933 has also been substantially revised.

I wish to express my gratitude to several friends, whose work has helped me to write this small volume: Jeremy Noakes, Richard Bessel, Jill Stephenson, Klaus Tenfelde and three colleagues sadly no longer with us: Tim Mason, Detlev Peukert and Bill Carr. The greatest influences on my view of the Third Reich have come from Hans Mommsen, whose friendship I value as much as his scholarship, and from a historian who had the misfortune to be my best man at two weddings: Ian Kershaw. His work on Nazi Germany has gone from strength to brilliance; and his support has been invaluable to me.

R.J.G. 1999

Foreword

Lancaster Pamphlets offer concise and up-to-date accounts of major historical topics, primarily for the help of students preparing for Advanced Level examinations, though they should also be of value to those pursuing introductory courses in universities and other institutions of higher education. Without being all-embracing, their aims are to bring some of the central themes or problems confronting students and teachers into sharper focus than the textbook writer can hope to do; to provide the reader with some of the results of recent research which the textbook may not embody; and to stimulate thought about the whole interpretation of the topic under discussion.

Glossary and list of abbreviations

BVP	Bayerische Volkspartei (Bavarian People's Party)
DAF	Deutsche Arbeitsfront (German Labour Front)
DAP	Deutsche Arbeiterpartei (German Workers' Party), a forerunner of NSDAP
DDP	Deutsche Demokratische Partei (German Democratic Party)
DNVP	Deutschnationale Volkspartei (German National People's Party or Nationalists)
DVP	Deutsche Volkspartei (German People's Party)
Freikorps	'Free Corps'. Armed units used to repress revolutionary upheavals in 1918–19
Gau	Nazi Party geographical area, ruled by a Gauleiter, a regional party leader
Gestapo	Geheime Staatspolizei (Secret State Police)
KdF	Kraft durch Freude (Strength through Joy)
KPD	Kommunistische Partei Deutschlands (German Communist Party)
NSBO	Nationalsozialistische Betriebszellenorganisation (National Socialist Organisation of Factory Cells)
NSDAP	Nationalsozialistische Deutsche Arbeiterpartei (National Socialist German Workers' Party or Nazis)

Reichskristall-nacht	Reich 'Crystal Night' or 'Night of Broken Glass', 9–10 November 1938 when synagogues and Jewish property were vandalised
Reichstag	the national parliament
Reichswehr	the army in the Weimar Republic
RGO	Rote Gewerkschaftsopposition (Red Trade Union Opposition or Communist union organisations)
SA	Sturmabteilung (storm troops)
SPD	Sozialdemokratische Partei Deutschlands (German Social Democratic Party)
SS	Schutzstaffeln (protection squads)
Wehrmacht	the armed forces in the Third Reich
ZAG	Zentralarbeitsgemeinschaft (Central Work Community: a forum for employer–trade union negotiations in the Weimar Republic)

1

Hitler: the man and his ideas

Adolf Hitler was born on 20 April 1889 in the small Austrian town of Braunau am Inn, where his father was a customs official. After five years at primary school, some time as an undistinguished pupil in Linz and experience as a boarder in Steyr, the apparently unremarkable Hitler, who never enjoyed his schooling (apart from his history lessons) and did not get on too well with his father, moved to Vienna in 1907. With sufficient support from relatives he remained for a time idle, doing little but daydream. The temporary end of such support led him to go through a short period of real hardship in 1909, when he lived rough, slept in the gutters and then found refuge in a doss house. Money from an aunt then put an end to this hardship; and Hitler made a living selling paintings and drawings of the Austrian capital and producing posters and advertisements for small traders. His two attempts to gain entry to the Academy of Graphic Arts failed, however, leaving the young Hitler an embittered man.

It was also while in Vienna that, by his own account, his eyes were opened to the twin menaces of Marxism and Jewry. The Jewish population of the Austrian capital (175,318) was larger than that of any city in Germany and included unassimilated and poor Jews from Eastern Europe. Anti-semitism was part of daily political discourse here; and in this regard Hitler learnt a great deal from the Viennese Christian Social leader Karl Lueger, who was for a time mayor of the city. Isolated, unsuccessful and with a marked distaste for the ramshackle and multinational Habsburg Empire, Hitler fled to Munich in 1913

1

to avoid service in the Austrian army. His flight was no simple act of cowardice, for, with the outbreak of war in August 1914, he rushed to enlist in the Bavarian army. He served with some distinction, being awarded the Iron Cross on two occasions and being promoted to lance-corporal in 1917. For him the war was a crucial formative experience. The 'Kamaraderie' of the trenches and sacrifice for the Fatherland were the values that Hitler was subsequently to contrast with the divisive and self-interested politics of the Weimar Republic. He was in hospital, recovering from a mustard-gas attack, when he learnt to his horror of Germany's defeat, the humiliation of the armistice and the outbreak of revolution in November 1918. Henceforth Hitler became a major proponent of the 'stab-in-the-back legend', the belief that it was not the army but civilian politicians who had let the nation down by signing the armistice agreement. Such politicians he denounced as 'November criminals'.

On leaving hospital Hitler returned to Munich, which experienced violent political upheavals in 1918 and 1919. Here he worked for the army, keeping an eye on the numerous extremist groups in the city. He soon came into contact with the nationalist and racist German Workers' Party (DAP), led by the Munich locksmith Anton Drexler. It rapidly became clear that Hitler was a speaker of some talent – at least to those who shared his crass prejudices. In October 1919 he made his first address to the DAP, won increasing influence in its councils and became one of its most prominent members. On 24 February 1920 the organisation changed its name to the National Socialist German Workers' Party (NSDAP). As both this new name and its programme made clear, the party was meant to combine nationalist and 'socialist' elements. It called not only for the revision of the Treaty of Versailles and the return of territories lost as a result of the peace treaty (parts of Poland, Alsace and Lorraine) but also for the unification of all ethnic Germans in a single Reich. Jews were to be excluded from citizenship and office, while those who had arrived in Germany since 1914 were to be deported, despite the fact that many German Jews had fought with honour on the German side during the First World War.

In addition to these staples of *völkisch* (nationalist/racist) thinking, the supposedly unalterable programme of the NSDAP made certain radical economic and social demands. War profits were to be confiscated, unearned incomes abolished, trusts nationalised and large department stores communalised. The beneficiary was to be the small man. (Note that this form of 'socialism' did not aim at the expropriation of all private property. Indeed, small businessmen and traders

2

were to be protected.) Even so, whether these socially radical aspects of the programme, so dear to the heart of Gottfried Feder, the party's 'economic expert', ever meant much to Hitler himself is open to doubt. In any case, by the late 1920s this aspect of Nazism was explicitly disavowed by Hitler, as the movement sought to win middle-class and peasant support. Hitler now made it clear that it was only *Jewish* property which would be confiscated. It was – somewhat paradoxically – the giant corporations, such as the chemical concern IG Farben, which were to prove the major financial beneficiaries of Nazi rule between 1933 and 1945.

During his time in Munich, Hitler also came into contact with various people who were subsequently to be of great importance to the Nazi movement. Some of these became his life-long friends: Hermann Göring, a distinguished First World War fighter pilot with influential contacts in Munich bourgeois society; Alfred Rosenberg, the ideologist of the movement; Rudolf Hess, who had actually served in Hitler's regiment during the war; and the Bechstein family of piano-makers. Among the most important of his associates at this time was Ernst Röhm of the army staff in Munich, who recruited former servicemen and Freikorps members (the Freikorps had been used to repress left-wing risings in 1918–19) into the movement and thereby established the Sturmabteilung or SA, the Nazi organisation of storm troopers, which was to increase the influence of the initially small party to a significant degree. All these people shared Hitler's view that Germany had been betrayed and was now confronted with a 'red threat'. They expressed a violent nationalist ardour that often encompassed racism and in particular anti-semitism. In 1922 Julius Streicher, the most vicious of the anti-semites, also pledged his loyalty to Hitler, bringing into the party his own Franconian organisation and thereby doubling its membership. In the same year the first intimations of the cult of the Führer, the idea that it was Hitler who was uniquely blessed to shape Germany's destinies, were seen.

At this time the NSDAP was but one of a plethora of extreme *völkisch* organisations in Munich (there were 73 in the Reich and 15 in the Bavarian capital alone). By 1923 it had links with the other four patriotic leagues in the Bavarian capital and was also in contact with the disaffected war hero General Ludendorff. Even the Bavarian state government under Gustav von Kahr was refusing to take orders from the national government in Berlin; and some of its members wanted to establish a separatist conservative regime, free from alleged socialist influence in the Reich capital, though they had no intention of including Hitler in any such arrangement. This tension formed the background to the attempted Beer Hall Putsch on the evening of 8 November 1923, which ended in farce in the face of a small degree of local resistance and the fact that the Reichswehr, the army, refused to join the putschists. In consequence the Nazi Party was banned and Hitler stood trial on a charge of high treason for his part in the attempt to overthrow Weimar democracy by force, receiving the minimum sentence of five years' imprisonment. This example of the right-wing sympathies of the German judiciary in the Weimar Republic was further compounded by the fact that Hitler, at this stage still not even a German citizen, was given an understanding that an early release on probation was likely. The trial created Hitler's national reputation in right-wing circles; and in any case he was released from the prison as early as December 1924, despite the severity of his crime. While in gaol in the small Bavarian town of Landsberg am Lech, however, he had dictated to a colleague the text of what became *Mein Kampf*.

Mein Kampf ('My Struggle') is scarcely one of the great works of political theory. Its style is crass and was in earlier editions ungrammatical. Free from subtleties of any kind, it repeats over and over again the most vulgar prejudices and blatant lies. It uses interchangeably words which in fact have different meanings (people, nation, race, tribe) and bases most of its arguments not on empirical evidence but on analogies (usually false ones). In so far as the book possesses any structure, the first part is vaguely autobiographical, the second an account of the early history of the NSDAP. As autobiography and history it is full of lies – about Hitler's financial circumstances in Vienna, which were nothing like as dire as he would have the reader imagine, about when he fled from Vienna and when he joined the German Workers' Party. It is important to note, however, that the strange style, the repetition of simplistic arguments and blatant untruths, in *Mein Kampf* was not simply a consequence of Hitler's intellectual deficiencies. He never claimed to be an intellectual and had nothing but contempt for them. What he was attempting in *Mein Kampf* was to render the *spoken* word, political demagogy, in prose. This was partly because Hitler was in prison when he dictated the work and therefore unable to address public meetings in person. (In fact the ban on his speaking publicly continued for some time after his release.) It was also, however, a consequence of his beliefs about the nature of effective propaganda.

A considerable part of *Mein Kampf* is devoted to reflections on the nature of propaganda. Hitler believed that one of the reasons for British success in the First World War was the fact that British propaganda had been superior to that of the imperial German authorities, superior in its simplicity, directness and willingness to tell downright lies. He had also been influenced by certain ideas about the susceptibility of the masses adduced by theorists such as the American MacDougall and the Frenchman Le Bon. What this thinking added up to was that the masses were swayed less by the written word than by the spoken, especially when gathered in large numbers in a public place. The way to win mass approval and gain mass support under such circumstances was neither by reference to factual details nor by logical sophistication. Rather the most effective route to the popular heart lay in the perpetual repetition of the most simple and vehement ideas. If you are going to lie, then tell the big lie and do not flinch from repeating it. This argument worked because, to Hitler, the masses were 'feminine'. In his sexist view, women were swayed not by their brains but by their emotions.

If such reflections explain perhaps a little of the deficiencies of *Mein Kampf* in terms of logic and literary elegance, what, then, of its content? Various issues are picked up in the work in no thorough or systematic fashion. One of these is the appropriate diplomatic and foreign aims of the German state. Hitler was always adamant that the humiliation of the Treaty of Versailles had to be overturned and the Reich's lost territories (Alsace, Lorraine and parts of Poland) returned to Germany. He was also aware that France would never surrender Alsace and Lorraine peacefully. Thus a coming war with France was already implicit in his thinking. However, Hitler's territorial ambitions did not end with the re-creation of the boundaries of Bismarck's Germany. Bismarck, after all, had deliberately excluded Austria and thereby Austrian Germans from the Reich that was created after the victories of 1866 and 1871. In contrast Hitler advocated the pan-German vision of a Reich which would include all ethnic Germans: he wanted *ein Volk, ein Reich* (one people, one empire). Despite the ostensible commitment of the US President Wilson and his victorious allies to the self-determination of peoples, such self-determination had been denied to the Germans at the end of the First World War. *Anschluss* (union) with the rump Austrian state was not permitted. At the same time the new states of Czechoslovakia and Poland contained significant German minorities. The ambition

5

to unite all ethnic Germans in a single Reich thus had highly disruptive implications for Central and Eastern Europe.

Even these pan-German aims, however, were not sufficient to satisfy Hitler. He further believed that the German people were being forced to live in a territorial area that was overcrowded and could not meet their needs. Such circumstances bred moral and political decay, especially as many of a nation's best qualities were to be found not in the cities but in the rural areas and among the peasantry. This became known as the ideology of *Blut und Boden* (blood and soil). What the German people needed was *Lebensraum* (living space). In turn this raised the question: where was such living space to be found? One answer might be in the possession of colonies; but Hitler quickly rejected such a solution. Colonies could not be easily defended and could be cut off from the Fatherland by naval action, exactly as had happened between 1914 and 1918. Any German bid for colonies was also likely to antagonise Britain, according to Hitler the very mistake that the imperial leadership had made before the First World War. Increasingly, therefore, he came to believe that *Lebensraum* would have to be found in the east of Europe and in Russia in particular, where foodstuffs and raw materials were also abundant. Here then was a programme which implied war in the east. In Hitler's view, such a war was to be welcomed. First, he subscribed to a crude form of social Darwinism, which claimed that wars between peoples were a natural part of history. Pacifism he dismissed as a Jewish invention! Second, a war against Soviet Russia would be a holy crusade against Bolshevism, a claim that had no little attraction, not only to many Germans, but also to conservatives throughout Europe. Third, a war against Russia would be a war of superior 'Aryans' (the term Hitler restricted incorrectly to the Nordic peoples) against both inferior Slavs and disastrous Jewish influence – for Bolshevism was yet another evil that Hitler considered to be a Jewish concoction. Indeed, he believed in the existence of an international Jewish conspiracy which embraced both international Marxism and international finance. Like many fellow anti-semites, Hitler thought that the existence of such a conspiracy had been demonstrated by *The Protocols of the Elders of Zion*, a document which was forged by the Tsarist secret police and intended to distract popular discontent away from the regime and towards the archetypal Jewish scapegoat.

The core of Hitler's obsessive beliefs and prejudices was a virulent racism, a vicious anti-semitism, set out in the chapter on 'People and Race' in *Mein Kampf*. Here Hitler stated that the peoples of the world could be divided into three racial groups: the creators of culture, the bearers of culture (people who can imitate the creations of the superior race), and inferior peoples who are the 'destroyers of culture'. Only 'Aryans' were capable of creating cultures, which they did in the following way: small groups of well-organised Aryans, prepared to sacrifice themselves for the communal good, conquered larger numbers of inferior people and brought to them the values of culture. (It is worthy of note that 'culture', another undefined term, is in this account created by the sword.) For a time all went well until the master race began to mix with its inferiors. This 'sin against the blood' led to racial deterioration and inevitable decay. As a result Hitler came to believe that the prime role of the state was to promote 'racial hygiene' and to prevent racial intermixing. Subsequently the Nazi state did embody these eugenic values, with vicious consequences for the 'impure'. Significantly the superiority of the Aryan resided, according to Hitler, not in the intellect but in the capacity for work, the fulfilment of public duty, self-sacrifice and idealism. He believed that these qualities were not created by society but were genetically determined.

For Hitler the opposite of the Aryan was the Jew. Again it is significant that he explicitly denied that Jewishness was a matter of religion; rather it was inherited: that is, biologically determined. Historically a great deal of European anti-semitism had been generated by the Christian denunciation of the Jews as the murderers of Christ. Unpleasant and murderous as the consequences of this religious form of anti-semitism had often been, it had nonetheless regarded those Jews who converted to Christianity as no longer Jewish. In the pseudo-scientific, biological anti-semitism of the Nazis, on the other hand, such a possibility was excluded: once a Jew, always a Jew. And, for Hitler, being a Jew meant the invariable possession of those traits which made the Jew the opposite of the Aryan: possessing no homeland – what would Hitler have made of the existence of the state of Israel today? – the Jew was incapable of sacrificing himself for a greater, communal good; he was materialistic and untouched by idealism. Through international finance and international Marxism the Jew attempted to subvert real nations and in fact became parasitical upon them. The use of parasitical analogies reached horrendous proportions in Hitler's thinking: Jews were likened to rats, vermin, disease, the plague, germs, bacilli. Almost anything that Hitler disliked was blamed on the Jews: the decisions of both Britain and the United States to fight against Germany during the First World War;

7

Germany's defeat in that war; the Russian Revolution; international Marxism; the rapacious banks; and the terms of the Treaty of Versailles. The language used to denounce the Jews was significant: portrayed in *inhuman* terms, Jews did not have to be treated as human beings. If Jews were 'vermin', then they were to be treated as such: that is, eradicated. *Mein Kampf* spoke darkly of the 'extermination' of 'international poisoners' and reflected that the sufferings of Germans in the First World War would not have been in vain had Jews been gassed at its inception.

So far we have seen that the ideas expressed in *Mein Kampf* involved the possibility of war in west and east, and policies of racial hygiene and anti-semitism. They were also clear that the Nazi state would not be democratic. For Hitler democratic competition between political parties was self-interested horse-trading. Democratic politics brought out the divisions within a nation rather than unity and would not prove sufficiently strong to resist the threat of communism. What was needed, therefore, was a strong leader, a *Führer*, who would recognise and express the popular will and unite the nation behind him in a 'people's community' (*Volksgemeinschaft*), in which old conflicts would be forgotten.

The various ideas that appear in *Mein Kampf* have raised two particular questions for historians: first, were such ideas the product of a deranged mind or, if not, what were their origins? Second, did these ideas constitute a programme that was systematically implemented in the Third Reich? In terms of the origins of Hitler's anti-socialist and anti-semitic obsessions, and of his territorial ambitions, few historians have been prepared to dismiss him as simply mad. Much psychological speculation rests on a few shreds of miscellaneous evidence or on none at all. What is more, much of this evidence has been provided by people with axes to grind and scores to settle. This is not to say that Hitler was not obsessive about certain things, nor that he was never neurotic. He was a hypochondriac and extremely fastidious about his food, becoming a vegetarian in the early 1930s. He was preoccupied with personal cleanliness. Most markedly, he possessed an unshakable belief in his own rightness and destiny, found it difficult to accept contradiction and had nothing but contempt for intellectuals. He could be enormously energetic at certain times, yet was often indolent (with consequences that will be explored later). Somewhat remote, he did not make friends easily but enjoyed the company of women. On the other hand, when he did make friends he remained extremely loyal to them, especially towards those who had been with him in the early days in Munich. It is true that Hitler sometimes appeared to behave in a manic way, as in the tantrums of rage thrown before foreign leaders or in the clippings seen so often by British audiences of his apparently hysterical public speeches. Much of this, however, was misleading. Hitler's speeches were carefully planned; indeed, he practised his gestures in front of the mirror. Furthermore the speeches normally began quietly and slowly. The apparent hysteria at the end was thus planned and instrumental; and the same could be said of many, if not all, of his tantrums. It is true that towards the end of the war the Führer increasingly lost touch with reality; but, considering that he was living in remote forests, growing dependent on drugs for the treatment of ailments real or imagined and confronted with by then insuperable problems, this is scarcely surprising. In none of this is there the slightest suggestion of clinical madness.

In any case, one does not need to speculate upon the psychological consequences of Hitler's experience of mustard gas during the First World War or certain physical peculiarities (the failure of one testicle to drop) or a supposedly 'sado-masochistic' personality in order to locate or understand the origins of his ideas, however evil they may have been. Sad as it may be, *völkisch* and anti-semitic prejudices were far from uncommon in Austria before the First World War; and it was significant that Hitler came from Austria rather than the more western parts of Germany. Indeed, many of the leading antisemites in the NSDAP, including the theorist Alfred Rosenberg, who came from the Russian town of Reval, were 'peripheral Germans'. For race was an issue of much greater importance in Eastern Europe, where national boundaries did not overlap with ethnic ones. The pan-German movement emerged in Austria in the late nineteenth century under the leadership of Georg von Schönerer, whose ideas had a considerable impact on the young Hitler. In part pan-Germanism, the demand for a single country for all Germans, was a response of Germans within the Austro-Hungarian Empire to the growing national awareness of other ethnic groups, among them Poles and Hungarians, with a historical nationhood, and others such as Czechs and Serbs seeking at the very least greater autonomy and in some cases independence. The virulence of popular anti-semitism in eastern Europe was equally a response to the fact that the Jewish presence there was much more marked than in Germany, where there were no huge ghettos and where Jews constituted less than 1 per cent of the total population. Racial hatred was further fuelled in the eastern parts of Europe by the fact that many of the Jews there were unassimilated, dressed distinctly and remained loyal to their own traditions. Hitler's account of encountering a Jew on the streets of Vienna makes great play of the latter's wearing of a caftan and ring-locks. (It should also be noted that ideas about racial hygiene were not restricted to Hitler, nor, for that matter, to Central Europe. Originating in England and adopted with some enthusiasm in the United States and Scandinavia, the idea of sterilising the infirm and degenerate was widespread in the 1920s.) Other influences on Hitler's anti-semitism, however, were more 'German'. This applies in particular to the views of the Bayreuth circle – to some extent to those of Richard Wagner himself but even more to those of his family survivors, admirers and Houston Stewart Chamberlain – who embraced what Saul Friedländer has described as a 'redemptive anti-semitism', a belief that the redemption of the Aryan required the eradication of the Jew.

The extent to which *Mein Kampf* constituted some kind of plan for policies later implemented by the Nazis is much more problematical. It is the case that Hitler unleashed a world war, destroyed parliamentary democracy and led a state that embarked upon the policies of racial genocide. Thus it is easy to understand why many historians have regarded the Third Reich and its barbarism as the inevitable consequences of the views that Hitler had long expressed. Recently, however, some analysts of government in Germany between 1933 and 1945 have moved away from such an 'intentionalist' explanation of Nazi policy and have come to stress 'structural' constraints on policy and the chaotic nature of decision-making. For Hitler was often unwilling or unable to reach decisions, especially where they might have a deleterious effect on his popularity. Against this background, as Ian Kershaw has written, Hitler's ideology has been seen less as a 'programme' than as a loose framework for action, which was only gradually translated into 'realisable objectives'. (This debate will be explored at greater length in Chapter 3.) Suffice it to say that, even if *Mein Kampf* was not a blueprint for a specific course of action (and there are good reasons to doubt that it was), it was nonetheless a 'framework for action', often for action on the part of people and agencies who *believed* they were implementing the wishes of the Führer.

When Hitler emerged from prison in December 1924 his position among the various right-wing groups in Germany was relatively strong. His performance at the trial was widely admired in nationalist circles, while the Nazi Party was in a state of crisis during his imprisonment, banned by law and lacking strong leadership. The dramatic failure of the Beer Hall Putsch convinced Hitler that the road to power lay through the democratic process, even though his ultimate aim remained the destruction of parliamentary democracy. This insight he brought to the party at its refounding in Munich on 27 February 1925, when the ban on the NSDAP expired. Enhanced as Hitler's status may have been within the extreme right of German politics, his position was at this stage still confronted by serious challenges. Apart from a series of bitter personal clashes between leading figures in the Bavarian party, the most serious threat came from the Gauleiter of northern and western Germany, under the leadership of Gregor Strasser. They were concerned to stress the socially radical aspects of Nazism and to this end demanded a new party programme. Such a demand Hitler saw as a threat to his leadership; and at a party meeting in the Franconian town of Bamberg (northern Bavaria) on 14 February 1926 he successfully saw off the challenge, stressing his commitment to the original programme and demanding loyalty to the Führer. Henceforth Hitler's position within the Nazi movement was impregnable; and even former critics such as Joseph Goebbels, who had stood on the left of the movement and was at one stage committed to 'national Bolshevism', were won over. From now on much effort was devoted to the reorganisation of the party and the creation of groups of activists throughout Germany. At the same time the few remaining independent *völkisch* groups were swallowed up by the NSDAP.

Despite successes *within* the extreme right, however, Hitler was still far removed from the centre of Weimar politics. The policies of the Nazi Party held little attraction for most German voters at this time. This was demonstrated quite clearly in the Reichstag elections of 1928, when the party gained only 2.6 per cent of the popular vote. It did win almost 10 per cent of the vote in some Protestant rural regions of north-west Germany in 1928 (Schleswig-Holstein and Lower Saxony), but few could have guessed what significance this would have for the future. The result of the 1928 elections brought to power a coalition government, the so-called 'Grand Coalition', embracing the German Social Democratic Party (SPD), a major winner in the elections, and various middle-class parties. Within two years this coalition had collapsed and thereafter the Reichstag was impotent, for it became impossible to construct viable coalition majorities with Nazi and Communist gains at the polls. At the same time the NSDAP emerged as the largest single party in the country.

In November 1928 Hitler, again allowed to speak in public in several German states, received an enthusiastic welcome from students at Munich University. Subsequently the NSDAP registered significant successes in student union elections (32 per cent in Erlangen, 20 per cent in Würzburg). More significantly, the party broke the 10 per cent barrier in votes cast in the Thuringian state election of December 1929, mainly at the expense of the DVP, the DNVP and the agrarian Landbund. This was little, however, in comparison with the fortunes of the party in the following year, when the NSDAP won 6,379,000 votes (18.3 per cent of the electorate) in national elections. In Schleswig-Holstein its share of the vote went up to 27 per cent. In rural Oldenburg the party won 37.2 per cent of all votes cast in May 1931 and 37.1 per cent in Mecklenburg in November of the same year. Three-quarters of the Nazi electorate were at this stage non-Catholic and they lived mainly in rural areas. The first seven months of 1932 witnessed the peak of Nazi success before Hitler became Chancellor. In July 1932 the NSDAP won over 6 million votes (37.4 per cent). At the same time its membership soared to 1.4 million.

The massive transformation of party fortunes in such a short time suggests that Nazi success was not simply a consequence of the party's propaganda or Hitler's charisma, important as these were, but really depended upon the climate within which Weimar politicians operated.

2

Weimar and the rise of Nazism

Many traditional accounts of the collapse of the Weimar Republic and the rise of Nazism list the host of difficulties which faced the fledgling democracy during its short existence (albeit not as short as that of the Third Reich!). Among these were the diplomatic and economic difficulties engendered by the Treaty of Versailles, problems which stemmed from the new constitution, the absence of a democratic consensus, the inflation in the early years of the Republic and the slump at its end. In this account the problems of the Weimar government just piled one on top of the other until the final straw broke the camel's back. Such an approach has much to commend it; and certainly all the problems listed above were real ones. Yet a word of caution should be introduced here: not all of these problems were encountered simultaneously. For example, the early years of the Weimar Republic witnessed inflation and then the ravages of hyperinflation, whereas the depression of 1929–33 was a time *not* of rising but of falling prices. This raises some extremely important chronological questions: why was the new state able to survive inflation and not depression? Why did it collapse in the early 1930s and not between 1919 and 1923? Why was the Nazi Party in the political wilderness until the late 1920s? Clearly such questions cannot be answered by a list of difficulties that fails to take into account the timing of their occurrence.

There can be no doubt that the Weimar Republic was born under difficult circumstances, indeed in circumstances of defeat and national humiliation. This alone was sufficient to damn it in the eyes of the

German right, which denounced democratic and socialist politicians for 'stabbing Germany in the back'. The fears of the nationalists were further compounded by the German Revolution of November 1918 and by the subsequent emergence of a mass communist movement. Their anger knew no bounds when the conditions of the *Diktat* (the dictated terms of the peace agreement) of Versailles became known in the summer of 1919. According to the terms of that treaty, the Central Powers (Germany and Austria-Hungary) were exclusively responsible for the outbreak of war in August 1914. Germany was to pay the victorious *Entente* Powers huge financial reparations, which compounded the country's already vast economic problems. In addition Germany's colonies were handed over to the victors, while some of the eastern territories were ceded to Poland, driving a corridor between East Prussia and the rest of Germany. Alsace and Lorraine were returned to France. These losses were not just a matter of pride: parts of Silesia incorporated in the new Polish state had valuable lignite deposits. Alsace hada highly developed textile and engineering industries and Lorraine possessed rich deposits of iron ore that had provided cheap raw material for the steel industry of the Ruhr. The Treaty of Versailles confiscated the German mercantile marine and would have done the same with the German navy, had not its sailors scuttled the battle fleet at the Scottish naval base of Scapa Flow. To prevent the resurgence of German militarism, the size of the army was also restricted. Finally the Treaty of Versailles did not accord to the German people the same right of self-determination that was extended to the Poles and the Czechs. Germany and Austria were not allowed to join together in a single state or customs union; while several of the new states included a German minority among their citizens, most notably in the case of the Sudetenland in northern Czechoslovakia. Needless to say, the Treaty of Versailles fuelled nationalist propaganda; and even in the rest of Europe there were those who believed that Germany had been too harshly treated. Such a belief partly explains the British and French policies of appeasement in the late 1930s.

Faced with these facts, it would be impossible to deny that the terms of the Treaty of Versailles played a major role in the collapse of the Weimar Republic. It was a constant factor in the rhetoric of the German National People's Party (DNVP) and of the Nazis themselves. The renegotiation of reparations, which produced the Young Plan, was cause in 1929 for the Nazis and the Nationalists (DNVP) to join together in the Harzburg Front to organise a plebiscite against it.

This development has often been seen as important for subsequent Nazi success, in so far as Hitler, the extremist politician, was now seen centre stage with leading conservatives and accorded a hitherto unprecedented degree of respectability. Reparations continued to be denounced by some German businessmen as one of the causes of their problems, though it should be noted that a majority of the industrial community wanted the Young Plan signed and out of the way, so that international trade could resume. Financial problems engendered by reparations continued to bedevil the formulation of national economic policy throughout the Republic's existence.

Yet this was not the whole story. Certain questions still remain about the role and significance of the Treaty of Versailles for the survival of Weimar democracy. In the first place, the Nationalists (the DNVP), led from 1928 by Alfred Hugenberg, were as hostile to the treaty as the Nazis. Thus the greater electoral success enjoyed by the latter requires an explanation additional to nationalism and Versailles. Second, if Versailles were so important, why did the new Republic not collapse earlier, when both the defeat and the treaty were at their most immediate? Why did the political system of Weimar crumble when many of the actual economic problems of reparations were less pressing – they had been regularised and reduced by the Dawes and Young plans – than in 1923, when the French and Belgians occupied the Ruhr to exact payment forcibly? Why, above all, did coalition governments hold together when dealing with the reparations issue and Versailles, and yet collapse in 1929–30 over a much more mundane issue, that of unemployment benefits and who should pay for them? It was also the case that most German businessmen, especially those with international trading connections and large export markets, were in favour of signing the Young Plan as quickly as possible to regularise trade relations. For businessmen, taxation and insurance costs were of much greater significance to them than Versailles.

Similar reservations can be expressed about another matter that has been held harmful to the Weimar Republic, namely its constitution. Two aspects of the constitution have been signalled for particular criticism: on the one hand, the powers accorded to the President of the Republic and, on the other, the introduction of absolute proportional representation. In the first case the constitution gave the President power to rule by emergency decree and thus dispense with the need for parliamentary majorities when he deemed the country to be in some kind of danger. With the collapse of the Grand Coalition

15

in 1930 and the appointment of Brüning as Chancellor, this is what happened: presidential cabinets governed and their wishes were authorised by the aged and conservative President Hindenburg. Second, the introduction of absolute proportional representation had a number of consequences. If a party could get even 2 per cent of the popular vote, it would be awarded 2 per cent of the seats in parliament. Thus small parties, such as the NSDAP in its early days, could get off the ground and survive in a way that would simply not have been possible in Britain under a first-past-the-post electoral system. Furthermore absolute proportional representation encouraged a proliferation of political parties and made it more or less impossible for any one party to obtain an absolute majority in the Reichstag. Government was therefore invariably by coalition; and the construction of coalitions was never easy, given the sheer multiplicity of parties with parliamentary seats (over 20 in the 1928 Reichstag). Again, however, some words of caution are necessary.

The first President of the Republic, the Social Democrat Friedrich Ebert, had, like his successor Hindenburg, the power to govern through emergency decree; but he used this power to protect the young state against putsches from the right and insurrections from the left. So the personal and political views of the President were of some importance, independent of the power of emergency decree. In any case the use of these decrees by Hindenburg came *after* the coalition system had already broken down and after – not before – it had proved more or less impossible to construct a parliamentary majority. This again leads us back to the question of timing: why did parliamentary government collapse when it did? The answer is not to be found in the constitution. As far as the electoral system is concerned, it is beyond dispute that absolute proportional representation led to the fragmentation of party politics. Yet it is worth remembering that imperial Germany had produced a multi-party system even before the First World War and despite the fact that there was no system of proportional representation then. In fact many parties in the Weimar parliament could claim ancestry from several of these pre-war parties. It is also worthy of note that there were times, especially between 1924 and 1928, when coalition government did manage to function. Yet again, therefore, the question of chronology cannot be avoided. (The British prejudice against governmental coalitions should also not be allowed to obscure the fact that such governments have enjoyed great stability in Germany and Scandinavia since 1945.)

In this context it may not have been so much the number but rather the nature of political parties in the Weimar Republic that really mattered. First, many of the parties were closely aligned with specific economic interest groups. The SPD, for example, was primarily concerned to represent its working-class membership and electorate, and had close links with the Free Trade Unions. The German People's Party (DVP), on the other hand, was closely aligned with big business interests. This would not have prevented successful coalition politics in times of economic prosperity or when foreign policy issues predominated. It was fatal, however, in the circumstances of depression, when declining business profitability led the DVP to argue for a relaxation of tax burdens and social welfare payments, at the same time as the SPD demanded an increase in state funding for the growing mass of the unemployed. It was precisely the inability of these two parties to agree on this issue of unemployment relief that caused the Grand Coalition to collapse in 1929–30, ushering in a period of presidential rule.

A second aspect of German party politics boded ill for the stability of parliamentary democracy after the First World War. Quite simply, many parties never accepted the democratic system. The Nationalists looked back nostalgically to the semi-autocratic state of the imperial period, while the DVP was prepared to work within the system but was never committed to it as a matter of principle. The German Communist Party (KPD) denounced Weimar democracy as a capitalist sham, to be overthrown by proletarian revolution. Only the labour wing of the Catholic Centre Party, the German Democratic Party (DDP) and the SPD were fully committed to upholding the democratic system. From 1928 onwards the situation became even more dire in terms of the absence of a democratic consensus. The DNVP became even more reactionary under the leadership of Hugenberg, the national leadership of the Centre Party moved to the right, and the DVP contained elements which preferred government by presidential cabinets to the parliamentary process.

Another factor which contributed little to the survival of Weimar was perpetual economic and financial difficulty. The first economic problem was occasioned by the transition to a peacetime economy in 1918–19. The demobilisation of 7 million soldiers and the running down of the war industries created unemployment. In the winter of 1918–19 over 1 million Germans were without jobs. Compared with later levels of unemployment, this figure does not look high. It was important, however, that the unemployed were concentrated in a relatively few large cities (over a quarter of a million in Berlin alone in January 1919), which were already politically volatile. Some of those who participated in the so-called Spartacist Rising (a left-wing insurrection) in Berlin in early January 1919 were jobless. More important, however, was the remarkably rapid disappearance of unemployment in the post-war boom which Germany enjoyed from the spring of 1919 to the middle of 1923. Now the problem changed: Germans were confronted first with high levels of price inflation and then with stupendous hyperinflation. Between 1918 and 1922 prices rose at a rate that often outstripped rises in nominal wages; thus the purchasing power of many declined. This formed the background to a massive wave of strikes between 1919 and 1922 and to the rise of extremist politics. The hyperinflation of 1923, however, was something else again. Money became worthless, not even worth stealing. Those on fixed incomes – pensioners, invalids, those dependent on their savings, *rentiers* – were ruined; and although those on wages fared somewhat better, as such wages were regularly re-negotiated, prices still rose faster than pay. It is not surprising, therefore, that inflation has often been seen as the nail that sealed Weimar's coffin. It certainly alienated some of its victims from the system permanently and may explain why the NSDAP won disproportionate support among pensioners in the late years of the Republic (though reductions in rates of support between 1930 and 1932 were again probably more important in this context). Here once again the question of the timing of the Republic's collapse becomes relevant.

Despite attempted right-wing *putsches* in Berlin and in Munich in 1920 and 1923 respectively, despite communist attempts to seize power in 1919, 1921 and 1923 in various parts of Germany, and despite the havoc wrought by inflation and even hyperinflation, the Weimar Republic survived. When it collapsed, in the early 1930s, the problem in economic terms was *not* inflation. In the Depression prices were actually falling. This suggests that the inflationary period was not one of unmitigated disaster for all Germans. Working out who won and lost from the inflation is far from easy; for many people were both debtors (beneficiaries as the inflation wiped out their debts) *and* creditors (losers as inflation meant they could not reclaim the real value of what they had lent to others). Also the courts did manage to organise some forms of recompense for former creditors. Although there can be no doubt that there were real losers, in particular those on fixed incomes, it is equally true that there were some whose position was actually helped by price inflation. This was especially true of primary producers. Although the farming

18

community complained about many things, particularly government attempts to control food prices, between 1919 and 1923, it generally stayed away from right-wing extremist politics in the early years of the Republic. After 1928 the Nazis notched up some of their first and most spectacular electoral successes in the rural areas of Protestant Germany. Part of the reason for this change was that both large land-owners and small peasant farmers saw their incomes rise between 1919 and 1922 with high food prices. For them it was falling agricultural prices in later years and a massive crisis of indebtedness in the early 1930s that were to prove a disaster.

Big business did not regard the inflationary period as an unmitigated disaster either. Inflation wrote off the debts incurred in earlier borrowing from the banks. The fact that the price of goods rose faster than did nominal wages effectively reduced labour costs; while the devaluation of the mark on international money markets meant that German goods were very cheap abroad and that foreign goods were extremely expensive in Germany. The result was high demand for German goods at home and abroad. Ironically the inflation prolonged Germany's post-war boom to 1923, whereas it had ended in Britain and France by 1921. A further consequence was that German business enjoyed very high levels of profitability until 1923. Some leading industrialists, such as Hugo Stinnes, actually encouraged the Reichsbank to print more paper money in consequence. (This inflationary strategy had the further advantage that reparations were paid off in a devalued, almost worthless currency.) High business profitability also had consequences in the field of industrial relations. Forced to recognise trade unions in the wake of the 1918 Revolution and afraid of the threat of socialist revolution, employers were prepared to make concessions to organised labour of a kind unimaginable before 1914, when most had adopted authoritarian attitudes and refused to deal with trade unions. In the changed circumstances after the war, agreements were reached on union recognition, national wage rates and a shorter working day. Trade-union leaders and business representatives met in a forum called the Central Work Community (ZAG). Although such co-operation was imposed by fear of outside intervention, it was also made possible by the high levels of profitability enjoyed by leading companies in the early years of the Republic.

So, paradoxically, the inflation did not ruin the farming community and was in many ways not detrimental to the interests of big business. Things only got out of hand when the rate of inflation overtook the international devaluation of the mark in 1923. This, together with

19

the occupation of the Ruhr, led to a massive collapse in the second half of the year, in which many firms went bankrupt and others were forced to lay off large numbers of workers. In the winter of 1923–24 the 'stabilisation crisis' saw unemployment rise to over 20 per cent of the labour force, which in turn led to an increase in political radicalism and a great upturn in the fortunes of the German Communist Party.

The period 1924 to 1928 used to be regarded as the 'golden years' of the Weimar Republic. Germany was admitted to the League of Nations and the foreign policy of Gustav Stresemann earned international recognition and respect. Inflation was conquered and economic output grew. The extreme right figured nowhere in mainstream politics in these years and coalition government did not seem to be a complete disaster. Yet historians have become increasingly aware of a series of problems in the 'tarnished' (rather than 'golden') 1920s. Politically the position of the traditional 'bourgeois' parties (DNVP, DVP, DDP), which had often been controlled by small groups of local notables, was eroded. In Schleswig-Holstein and Lower Saxony peasants deserted the DNVP, which was seen as representing the interests of large landowners, and formed their own special interest parties for a time. The lower middle class (*Mittelstand*) of the towns did much the same. Both groups subsequently turned to the Nazis in large numbers. On the economic front Germany's recovery had become disturbingly dependent upon foreign loans, on American capital in particular. This meant that the country was exceptionally vulnerable to movements on international money markets and highly dependent on the confidence of overseas investors. The Wall Street Crash of October 1929 made this fragility abundantly clear. Other problems were less directly linked to financial markets. Agricultural prices, which had begun to stabilise after the early 1920s, were already falling by 1927 and collapsed in the depression of 1929–33. The result was a crisis of indebtedness for farmers, whose alienation from the Republic was already forming in the 1926–28 period. The agrarian crisis fuelled a campaign of rural violence against tax collectors and local government and led to the first significant gains of the NSDAP in the agricultural areas of Schleswig-Holstein and Lower Saxony in 1928. These somewhat unexpected gains led the Nazis to reconsider their strategy, for much of their electoral propaganda had previously been directed at the urban working class, but with little reward. Although the NSDAP did not abandon agitation in the towns after 1928, it did switch its emphasis away from workers. In the towns the middle class was now targeted; but above all there was a concentration on rural areas and agricultural problems. This reaped huge dividends in the Reichstag election of 1930.

Nor was everything rosy in the industrial sector in the mid-1920s. Heavy industry (coal, iron and steel) was already experiencing problems of profitability: even in the relatively prosperous year of 1927 German steel mills worked at no more than 70 per cent of their capacity. The disaffection of iron and steel industrialists was demonstrated quite clearly in the following year, when a major industrial dispute took place in the Ruhr and the employers locked out over a quarter of a million workers. If some sections of big business were not exactly satisfied with their economic situation even in the mid-1920s, the same could also be said of some sections of German labour. It is true that the real wages of workers increased in the period 1924–28, but these gains were made at a certain cost. The introduction of new technologies associated with serial production (most obviously where conveyor belts were introduced, but elsewhere too) meant an intensification of labour, and an increase in the pace of work and in the number of industrial accidents. Even where no thorough process of technological modernisation took place – and this was true of most industries – work was subject to increasingly 'scientific management', a development sometimes described as 'Taylorism'. This meant increased controls on how workers spent their time on the shop floor, an increase in the division of labour and a speeding-up of work processes. Associated with this economic 'rationalisation' was the closure of small and inefficient units of production. A consequence of this development was the onset of *structural,* as well as the usual seasonal and cyclical, unemployment. After 1924 many were without jobs, even in the years of apparent prosperity: the annual average number of registered unemployed stood at over 2 million in 1926, 1.3 million in 1927 and nearly 1.4 million in 1928. Politically the major beneficiary of this unemployment was the KPD, which remained strong in many industrial regions such as the Ruhr and Berlin, even in the supposedly 'good' years of the mid-1920s.

The onset of the world economic crisis in 1929 made the problems of Weimar's middle years seem almost trivial. Agricultural indebtedness reached endemic proportions; and the Nazi promises to protect agriculture against foreign competition, to save the peasant and to lower taxes fell on ready ears. Big business entered a crisis of profitability, which made it increasingly antagonistic to welfare taxation and trade-union recognition, though hostility to the Republic should

21

not necessarily be equated with support for the Nazis. Now it could not afford, or so it claimed, the wage levels and concessions it had been prepared to make in the early years of the Republic, albeit under duress. Attempts to revive the ZAG met with no success. Falling prices dented the viability of many companies and led in some cases to bankruptcy, in others to the laying-off of workers *en masse*. At the nadir of the depression in April 1932 the official figure for the number of unemployed, probably an underestimate, stood at no fewer than 6 million, that is approximately one in three of the German labour force. (The consequences of this situation for the Weimar Republic's working class will be discussed in due course.) If the discontent of big business was bound to grow during the depression, the same was even more true as far as small businesses were concerned. Without the larger resources of the giant trusts, the smaller operators were especially vulnerable to falling prices. They also felt threatened both by big business and large retail stores, which could undercut them, and by organised labour, which was seen as being responsible for pushing up wages and as a threat to the small property owner. These were the fears of the German *Mittelstand* of small businessmen, shopkeepers, independent craftsmen and the self-employed, which were exploited with great success by Hitler and his followers. There is little doubt that the Protestant lower middle class provided a solid core of Nazi support.

So far we have seen that the Weimar Republic lived in the shadow of defeat, the Treaty of Versailles, constitutional difficulties, fragmented party politics, the absence of a democratic consensus, and a series of economic problems, of which the last – the depression – probably goes further towards explaining the precise timing of the collapse of the Republic than anything else. However, it does not in itself explain the specific political choices made by many Germans. It is all too easy to move from a list of political and economic difficulties to the assumption that the rise of Nazism and the triumph of Hitler were inevitable, that the difficulties led 'Germans' to look for some kind of saviour in the person of the Führer. Yet we must beware of generalisations about Germans. The highest percentage of the popular vote won by the NSDAP before Hitler became Chancellor in late January 1933 was just over 37 per cent in July 1932. Even at this point, therefore, almost 63 per cent of German voters did *not* give their support to Hitler or his party. So generalisations about 'Germans', which are intended to explain Nazi support, simply will not do. Moreover, the 37 per cent electoral support in July 1932 was not sufficient

to bring Hitler to power: for in the prevailing system of absolute proportional representation, the NSDAP occupied only 37 per cent of
the seats in the Reichstag and did not have a majority. At the same
time Hindenburg made it clear that he was not inclined to appoint
as Chancellor the upstart Nazi leader, whom he described as the
'bohemian corporal'. In addition, and partly as a result of this, the fortunes of the NSDAP went into rapid decline after the July elections.
Between July and November 1932 the Nazis *lost* 2 million votes. In
the November election of that year the combined vote of the Social
Democrats and the Communists was actually higher than that gained
by Hitler and his followers. With one relatively insignificant exception, the Nazi vote continued to decline in local and regional elections
before Hitler became Chancellor, i.e. between November 1932 and
late January 1933. The Nazi Party found itself in a deep crisis in late
1932. It had massive debts, subscriptions to the party press were in
decline, conservative electors had become suspicious of NSBO
involvement in the Berlin transport workers' strike in November
1932 and Protestant voters disliked the negotiations with the Catholic
Centre Party that had taken place earlier the same year. In the November elections the participation rate dropped to less than 81 per cent, the
lowest since 1928, and significant sections of rural society stayed away
from the polls. Thus Hitler's appointment as *Reichskanzler* was not the
result of acclamation by a majority of the German people. Rather it
ensued from a series of political intrigues with Conservative elites,
who arguably found it easier to incorporate the Nazi leader in their
plans precisely because his position appeared less strong than it
had been in the summer of 1932. These intrigues will be described
later.

That only some, and indeed not even a majority of, enfranchised
Germans voted Nazi makes it imperative to discover which groups
within the nation were most susceptible to Nazi propaganda and to
Hitler's acknowledged talents as a speaker and propagandist. There
has been a massive amount of research on the social bases of Nazi sup-
port; and virtually all commentators are agreed upon the following.
First, Nazi electoral support was much stronger in Protestant than in
Catholic Germany. In urban Catholic Germany (Aachen, Cologne,
Krefeld, Moenchen-Gladbach) industrial workers usually remained
loyal to the Centre Party or switched their vote to the KPD. In
Catholic rural areas the Centre Party or its Bavarian counterpart, the
Bavarian People's Party (BVP), remained dominant. Nazi electoral
success in Bavaria was largely restricted to Protestant Franconia.

(As always, there were some exceptions to the general rule: in Silesia the Nazis did well in the Catholic towns of Liegnitz and Breslau, as they did in rural Catholic areas of the Palatinate and parts of the Black Forest.) In July 1932 the Nazi share of the vote was almost twice as high in Protestant as in Catholic areas. Moreover, votes for the Centre Party (1928: 12.1 per cent of the popular vote, 1930: 11.8 per cent, 1932 July: 12.5 per cent, 1932 November: 11.9 per cent) remained more or less stable and were scarcely dented by rising support for the NSDAP. The same applied to the BVP (3.1 per cent, 3.0 per cent, 3.2 per cent, 3.1 per cent). This professed loyalty to the specifically Catholic parties was even more marked among female than among male voters.

That Hitler and his followers were generally unsuccessful in attempts to attract support in predominantly Catholic districts reflects a much more general truth about the nature of Nazi support: it came primarily from areas without strong political, social, ideological or cultural loyalties. In Catholic, as in social-democratic, Germany, voters' loyalty to their traditional representatives was reinforced by a dense network of social and cultural organisations (trade unions, sports clubs, choral societies, educational associations and so on), as well as – in the Catholic case – by the pulpit.

Second, the NSDAP mobilised a large percentage of the electorate in Protestant rural districts. It made its first gains in 1928 in Schleswig-Holstein and Lower Saxony, even though its general performance was dire. By July 1932 the scale of its support in such areas indicates that this came not solely from small peasant farmers but from other sections of rural society too, such as some large landowners and many rural labourers. In general the Nazi share of the total vote was much higher in rural districts than in the urban centres. Indeed, the larger the town, the lower tended to be the percentage of the electorate voting for the NSDAP. In July 1932, when the party averaged 37.4 per cent of the vote in the nation as a whole, its vote in the big cities was a good 10 per cent lower.

As far as voting behaviour in the towns was concerned, the Nazis enjoyed more success in small or medium-sized towns than they did in the great cities. Again historians are generally agreed that one important element in their electoral support here came from the *Mittelstand*. However, historical research is no longer prepared to accept the old stereotype of the NSDAP as simply a party of the lower middle class. An analysis of electoral choices in the wealthier parts of Protestant towns and of the votes of those who could afford a holiday away from home has indicated that significant numbers of upper-middle-class Germans were prepared to cast their vote for Hitler, at least in July 1932. The Nazis also enjoyed considerable support among the ranks of white-collar workers, who formed an increasing percentage of the labour force (over 20 per cent by this time) and who were strongly represented in the membership of the NSDAP. Once again, however, old stereotypes have had to be reviewed in the light of research: white-collar workers in the public sector (*Beamte*) were apparently more likely than those in the private sector (*Angestellte*) to give their vote to Hitler. Within the private sector, white-collar workers with supervisory and clerical functions, as well as those working in retailing, were more strongly inclined to Nazism than those with technical functions. White-collar workers living in large industrial towns and from manual working-class backgrounds were relatively immune to the NSDAP's appeals and often supported the SPD, whereas those living in middle-class districts or in small provincial towns, as well as those whose origins were not in the manual working class, were more likely to be Nazi supporters.

Already, therefore, we have seen that Hitler's party had broad-based support. It should be noted also that large numbers of Germans were still employed in agriculture at this time (almost one-third of the labour force) and that the self-employed and white-collar workers were also numerous. We are thus some way towards understanding how the Nazis could achieve a significant percentage of the vote. However, there is a further factor in the equation and one that has been hotly disputed: the extent of working-class support for Nazism. The larger and more industrial the town, the lower the Nazi percentage of the vote, though this was more true of Berlin, Hamburg and the Ruhr than of the Saxon towns. Agricultural labourers were more likely to vote Nazi than city factory workers. Relatively few former KPD voters switched to the Nazis, despite a popular stereotype. Workers were far less likely than middle-class elements to be members of the NSDAP or vote for the party. When the SPD lost votes in the depression, some of these went to the Nazis in 1930 and July 1932, but the major beneficiaries of desertions from both social democracy and the urban Centre Party were the Communists. In any case, some of the SPD deserters who found their way to Nazism may well have been white-collar workers. The massive rise in the NSDAP vote between 1930 and 1932 left the combined SPD/KPD vote more or less solid, again suggesting that previously organised workers were more immune to Nazi propaganda than many other groups in German society. Elections to factory councils and trade-union membership figures further suggest that the working-class Nazi was not typical. The overall results of the factory council elections in 1931 saw only 710 representatives of the Nazi Factory Cell Organisation (NSBO) elected as against 115,671 Free Trade Unionists (SPD-oriented) and 10,956 mandates for the predominantly Catholic Christian trade unions. In January 1933 the NSBO had some 300,000 members, compared with 1 million Christian Trade Unionists and over 4 million Free Trade Unionists.

This is not the whole story, however. Research by Peter Manstein has suggested a working-class membership for the NSDAP of around 35 per cent (though this still means a gross over-representation of upper- and middle-class members). Conan Fischer has demonstrated a large manual working-class presence in the SA; while Detlev Mühlberger's survey of several German regions suggests wide variations in working-class membership from one district to another (from almost two-thirds in some places to under one-fifth in others). In general he finds that levels of working-class representation within the NSDAP have hitherto been understated. He does admit, however, that the percentages were likely to be higher among rural labourers and in small towns; and it is not insignificant that most of the towns he has looked at are relatively small or medium-sized. The electoral studies of Jürgen Falter conclude that roughly one in four workers voted Nazi in July 1932 and that 40 per cent of the NSDAP's vote came from the working class. William Brustein thinks that even this figure may be an underestimate. Claus-Christian Szejnmann has also identified substantial Nazi gains among working-class communities in Saxony, one of the traditional heartlands of the SPD.

It does seem clear that the Nazis were able to attract significant sections of the German working-class electorate. They were more likely to do so in areas of artisan or cottage industry, as in Plauen in Saxony or Pirmasens in the Palatinate, than in heavy-industrial districts such as the Ruhr or in areas dominated by factory production. They were more successful in winning working-class support in rural Germany and in small provincial towns than in the big cities. A sub-stantial number of women workers also voted Nazi in July 1932, as did former agricultural workers, workers for whom employment in industry was a secondary activity and commuters who worked in the towns but lived in the countryside. What these various groups of working-class Nazi voters had in common was a lack of traditions of union and/or socialist/communist mobilisation; for the centre of trade-union and left-wing political organisation had remained the large town. The sheer size of these previously under-organised groups of workers should not be underestimated. In the early 1930s agriculture still employed over one-fifth of the labour force; and one-third of all those employed in 'industry and handicrafts' were self-employed or worked in firms with fewer than five employees. Cottage industry was still prevalent in shoe manufacture in Pirmasens and in large parts of the Saxon textile industry, as well as in instrument and toy making. More than half of all those registered as 'workers' in the occupational census of 1925 lived in small towns or villages of under 10,000 inhabitants. Thus there existed significant potential for Nazi success without that success undermining traditional working-class support for the SPD or the KPD, which had been largely concentrated in the big cities. The NSDAP also won over another group of workers who had an unusual political tradition: workers who had voted National Liberal before the First World War and DNVP after it. They tended to be workers who lived in the company housing provided by paternalistic employers, such as Krupp in Essen, and who were members of company unions and were tied to their firms by company insurance schemes and pension benefits. Additionally some Nazi votes came from workers in the public utilities (gas, water, electricity), the postal services and transport. In these cases both the KPD and the NSDAP benefited from the fact that it was often SPD-led local and regional governments which had to cut the wages of their employees or lay them off in the depression (1929–33).

Despite the above, workers, who constituted some 54 per cent of the German labour force, according to Michael Kater, remained under-represented in both the membership and the electorate of the NSDAP. It was rural labourers above all other categories of wage earners who were most likely to vote for Hitler. The claim, on the other hand, that the manual unemployed turned in large numbers to Hitler and his supporters cannot be sustained. In the Ruhr town of Herne the NSDAP did least well in areas of high unemployment, often scoring under 13 per cent of the vote, even in July 1932. In such areas the KPD enjoyed enormous success (between 60 and 70 per cent of the vote). In the Reich more generally the unemployed were overwhelmingly concentrated in the large industrial cities, precisely where the Nazis polled less well. The work of Jürgen Falter and Thomas Childers shows that the NSDAP achieved little support from the manual unemployed, who were twice as likely to vote Communist.

This distribution of Nazi support raises several important questions. Why, for example, were the Nazis more successful in Protestant than in Catholic Germany? At least part of the answer lies in what has been said about those groups of workers most amenable to Hitler's message: the NSDAP was most successful where it did not have to cope with strong pre-existing ideological or organisational loyalties. Where these did exist, as in Social Democratic and Communist strongholds, it did far less well. The same applied to Germany's Roman Catholic community, strongly represented over decades by the Centre Party (or the BVP in Bavaria). Loyalty to the party was reinforced by a plethora of Catholic leisure organisations and by the pulpit, from which the NSDAP was sometimes denounced as godless. On the other hand, Nazi success in Protestant rural and middle-class Germany was facilitated by the fact that political loyalties there were either weak or non-existent. Here Hitler's message was able to get through because peasant communities in Schleswig-Holstein and Lower Saxony had *already* deserted the DNVP, and because the lower middle class in the towns also abandoned the traditional bourgeois parties and formed a host of specific-interest parties. It was from these that Hitler picked up much of his support in the early 1930s. The significance of tradition and social milieu is also evident in Szejnmann's work on Saxon voters. The Social Democrats in Leipzig and Dresden were successful in defending their positions against National Socialist incursions precisely because a high percentage of SPD voters in these towns were also members of the party and because there existed a dense network of Social Democratic leisure and cultural organisations. Where the percentage of members to voters and the density of social and cultural organisations was lower, as in Chemnitz and Zwickau, the Nazis were much more successful. In the Erzgebirge and the Vogtland, areas in Saxony of industrial villages and domestic industry, the SPD disintegrated almost completely for much the same reasons.

Two other variables in voting behaviour need to be assessed: generation and gender. The NSDAP has often and with reason been portrayed as a dynamic inspirer of youth and contrasted with the sclerosis of the traditional right. The youthful image of the NSDAP (and especially of the SA) certainly has some foundation. The party's membership was younger than that of other parties in the Republic; and, according to Jürgen Falter, the average age of those joining the NSDAP between 1925 and 1932 was slightly under 29. That the Nazis did well among new voters may also reflect the youthfulness of some of its electors; while the average age of the SA's streetfighters lay between 17 and 22 years. However, youth politics were not uniform but divided to some extent at least according to social class, religious beliefs and gender, just as did the voting behaviour of its elders. The young unemployed, for example, were much more likely to turn to the Communists. It is also true that the NSDAP enjoyed remarkable success with elderly voters. According to Thomas Childers, being a pensioner was the most effective of all predictors of Nazi voting. Not only did the NSDAP make a specific bid for the support of pensioners, the elderly, and war veterans, who had seen the value of their pensions and savings eroded, but these groups, especially elderly women, constituted the largest reservoir of previous non-voters in the early 1930s!

For most of the Weimar Republic women exercised their right to vote less frequently than men, especially in rural areas. When they did vote, they sometimes followed the lead of husbands and fathers, though not always. It is true that the female vote divided along lines of class, religious beliefs and region, just as did the male; but it nonetheless remained distinctive. By 1930, 3.5 million women voted for the SPD; and far fewer women than men deserted the party for the communists in the depression. On the other hand, very few women voted for the KPD. Conversely women were more likely than men to vote for parties close to the churches (DNVP if Protestant, Centre Party if Catholic). Until 1930 they were unlikely to vote Nazi; but this then changed. The gap between male and female voting in this regard narrowed quite markedly between 1930 and July 1932, when 6.5 million women cast their votes for the NSDAP. The probability is that these were women with few previous political ties. Where they came from the working class, they were likely to be non-unionised textile operatives or domestic workers.

The issues deployed by Nazi electoral propaganda to mobilise this support were many and various. Of these, almost all commentators agree that the most significant were nationalism, the denunciation of the Treaty of Versailles and anti-Marxism, though it should be noted that this last meant opposition not only to the Communists, but also to the SPD, the unions, labour law and welfare legislation. Aspects of this hostility even to welfarism will be discussed in more detail later. In most local studies and from the contemporary investigations of Theodore Abel it would appear that anti-semitism did *not* play a major role either in electoral propaganda or as a mobilising factor, despite the commitment of leading Nazis to this cause and its horrendous consequences in the Third Reich. However, if the Nazi appeal had relied solely on nationalist and anti–Bolshevik rhetoric, it is difficult to see why the NSDAP should have done so much better in winning support than the traditional Nationalists in the DNVP, whose message was equally nationalistic and as virulently hostile to the socialist threat. Part of the explanation, at least, is that the Nazis were able to combine the usual platitudes of the German right with a populist and anti-establishment message. The party was never implicated in government in the Weimar period and thus escaped the necessity of taking unpopular decisions, which even the DNVP had to do on occasion. Its leaders were relatively young and not associated with either the traditional social elite or the political establishment. The NSDAP also made promises to the small man, to the peasant farmer and small shopkeeper, of protection not only against the Marxists but also against big business and large stores. To big business, on the other hand, the NSDAP promised the demolition of the Weimar system of industrial relations, the destruction of the power of the trade unions and the restoration of management's right to manage. To women the Nazis promised the return to traditional moral and family values. Interestingly the parties that thought at least partly in terms of female emancipation – the SPD and especially the KPD – did least well among women voters.

It is clear that the Nazis were often promising different things to different people, sometimes things that were incompatible, especially in terms of economic policy. How was this possible? There were several contributing factors. One was the fact that the main element of electoral campaigning at the time was the local political meeting: there was not the instantaneous national media coverage, to which we have become accustomed today. Television did not exist. Radio was controlled by the government of the day and still limited to a relatively small number of households. Most newspapers were local or tied to specific political organisations. Another reason was the ease with which the various groups of Nazi supporters described above could unite around the major but general themes of NSDAP propaganda: nationalism, hostility to socialism and the political mess of Weimar, as well as traditional moral and family values. However, it is important to realise that the impact of that propaganda was not simply the result of Goebbels' skill in exploiting symbols and rallies or of Hitler's undeniable talent as a speaker. It was also the consequence of an electoral professionalism manifested in two particular ways: first, the fact that the Nazi message reached parts of Germany other parties did not reach; second, the targeting of specific interest groups with specific messages. In the first case the NSDAP sent its speakers, including some of its major figures, into rural districts and small towns, which had often been neglected by the older political parties. In the second its propaganda section trained its speakers to address local and concrete issues, such as the problems of agriculture in Schleswig-Holstein (pig prices) or the threat to small shopkeepers in Hanover created by the building of a Woolworth's store in the town. Thus its success was not the result just of the mouthing of general slogans or the supposed 'irrationality' of the masses but also of the fact that it addressed the immediate and specific material concerns of many Germans. William Brustein similarly argues that Nazi 'Keynesianism' addressed the problems of the unemployed, though the fact that most of the unemployed stayed away from Nazism renders such an explanation problematical in this case.

What is indubitably true is that the Nazis invested more time and effort in electioneering than any other party. In middle Franconia (northern Bavaria) alone they held 10,000 meetings during the run-up to the national elections of 1930. In April 1932 the NSDAP took the imaginative step of issuing 50,000 records of one of Hitler's speeches; and in the presidential elections Hitler gave no fewer than 25 major speeches between 16 and 24 April of the same year.

With all the support it could mobilise before Hitler became Chancellor, the NSDAP still fell short of an absolute majority and, as we have already seen, it entered a major crisis after July 1932. The myth of the party's invincibility had been shaken, the party was becoming short of funds, and, as Goebbels admitted, morale was at a low ebb. Yet by the end of January 1933 Hitler was Chancellor. What made his appointment possible was what might be described as a deal between the mass Nazi movement on the one hand – Hitler would never have been taken seriously but for the scale of his electoral support – and key conservative groups and politicians on the other. Formulated in a different way, it was not just Hitler and the Nazis who wanted to be rid of the Weimar Republic; the same was true of several elite groups who came to play an important role in decision-making between 1930 and 1933. The Revolution of November 1918 had failed to remove from office teachers, bureaucrats, judges and army officers who had served in the imperial period and were never enamoured of the values of parliamentary democracy. Judges handed out derisory sentences to right-wing assassins or conspirators, as in the case of Hitler himself after the

Beer Hall Putsch. Teachers in the *Gymnasien* (the German equivalent of grammar schools) and many university professors continued to preach imperial and nationalist values. The relationship between the officer corps and the Republic was strained from the very start, as was demonstrated by a right-wing attempt to seize power in 1920, the so-called Kapp Putsch, named after its high-ranking leader. For, although the army did not join the putschists, it refused to act against them. The large landowners east of the Elbe, the aristocratic Junkers, were no more favourably inclined to the Weimar system and continued to have considerable influence – in particular with President Hindenburg, who was one of their own. With the collapse of coalition government in 1930 and rule by presidential decree, the machinations of these pressure groups became increasingly important and ultimately led to Hitler becoming Chancellor.

The hostility of Junkers and army officers to the Weimar Republic was not just a case of conservative 'traditionalism', however, but was also related to quite modern and material concerns. Hostility to the Weimar Republic within the officer corps, for example, was often encountered in the case of younger and non-aristocratic technocrats. Their concern was not the restoration of tradition but the modernisation of the army. For them the problem was that such modernisation was not possible in a political system in which they had to compete for funding with the different claims made by Social Democrats and trade unionists. In short, they believed that Weimar was spending too much on welfare and not enough on arms. Equally, the worries of large landowners stemmed from the economic crisis and chronic indebtedness that had hit the agricultural community. However, they did not blame international market forces for their problems but rather the Weimar system. Privileged and protected before the First World War, they now had to compete with industrial and consumer interests and found themselves subject to taxation to pay for welfare reform: for the Weimar Republic under Social Democratic and Centre Party influence became a welfare state. It increased invalidity, sickness and pension benefits and introduced a system of unemployment insurance. Council houses were built in great numbers, as were public parks, stadiums and public baths. These benefits, which accrued primarily to the urban working class, had to be paid for by increases in taxation, which were greatly resented in rural areas. In 1932 German farmers were also worried by the prospects of a bilateral trade agreement with Poland, which brought the threat of more cheap agricultural imports. Thus the concerns of the influential military and agrarian elites were of a quite concrete and not necessarily 'traditionalist' nature.

The concerns of the German business community were not dissimilar. The relationship between big business and Nazism has long been controversial; but it does seem that certain things can be said with some degree of certainty, especially after the research of Henry Ashby Turner. First, the NSDAP did not need external funding from industrialists: its own activities (charging admission to meetings, the sale of cigarettes and mineral water) were in the main self-financing. Second, the behaviour of the iron and steel baron Fritz Thyssen, who did provide the Nazis with funds and actually became a party member, was not typical of the business community as a whole. More typical was that of the Flick concern, which gave money to virtually every political party apart from the SPD and the KPD as a kind of political insurance. Far more industrial funds found their way to the DNVP and the DVP than to the Nazi Party. Hitler's supporters were more likely to be found among small businessmen than among the great moguls of the industrial world. All this is true; but I would argue that questions about the relationship between individual industrialists and the NSDAP are perhaps less important than the fact that industry in general became increasingly resentful of and hostile to the Weimar Republic. Business claimed that welfare taxation was ruining it and that the trade unions had far too much power. This last complaint related to the fact that employers were obliged to recognise the unions; that collective wage agreements were legally binding; and that a system of state intervention in industrial disputes was held to have left wages artificially high. Further legislation imposed certain controls on management and was equally resented. The net result was that most of industry wanted to get rid of the Weimar system, even though it was neither necessarily, nor in its majority, Nazi. Although the role of business in the political intrigues of late 1932 and early 1933 was probably far less important than that of military and agricultural interests, which carried much more weight with President Hindenburg, businessmen nonetheless formed yet another group in German society unwilling to back the Republic in its hour of need.

The ability of various elite and pressure groups to influence decision-making in the last years of the Weimar Republic rested on the fact that parliamentary government had effectively broken down by 1930, that is, actually some time before the Nazi seizure of power. From 1928 until March 1930 Germany was governed by a precarious coalition led by the Social Democrat Hermann Müller, which included representatives of the Centre, the BVP, the DDP and even the DVP. This coalition had to handle the impact of the depression. Increasingly the SPD, influenced by its trade-union allies, and the DVP, strongly associated with certain big business interests, found themselves at loggerheads over economic and financial policy in general and, in particular, over how the unemployment insurance fund should be supported. Essentially, the SPD wished to retain welfare benefits, while the DVP thought priority should be given to cutting government expenditure. The consequence of this impasse was the resignation of the Müller cabinet on 27 March 1930. Thus ended the Republic's last parliamentary government; for the focus of decision-making now shifted from the Reichstag to President Hindenburg, and to those who had influence with him, in particular General Kurt von Schleicher, who had come to speak for the army in the political arena.

Neither Hindenburg nor Schleicher thought attempts to cobble together yet another unstable coalition sensible in March 1930. They wanted a return to firm and decisive government. As a result, the succeeding cabinets of the new Chancellor, Heinrich Brüning, did not have to rely on majority votes in parliament to pass legislation. In any case they could not have manufactured a parliamentary majority, especially after the NSDAP's and KPD's huge electoral gains in the elections of September 1930. However, they could get the President to sign emergency decrees. In this fashion Brüning pursued policies of cutting government expenditure and reducing welfare benefits, policies thought highly desirable by agrarian and business interests. Yet this system of rule by 'presidential cabinets' was fraught with difficulties because of its dependence on the goodwill of Hindenburg and his advisers. As the economic crisis deepened, fuelled by Brüning's deflationary policies, as agriculture became increasingly indebted and shrill in its demands for protection, and as most business found itself in a crisis of profitability, so the voices of those wishing to unseat the Chancellor became louder. Much of big business was not particularly unhappy with his performance but the barons of iron, steel and coal, especially hard hit by the depression, thought he had not gone far enough in dismantling progressive labour legislation and welfare taxation. The agrarian lobby, dominated by Junker estate owners, also began to agitate for Brüning's removal, putting the idea in the President's head that a plan to take over insolvent agricultural properties in the eastern provinces and re-colonise them was a form of 'agrarian Bolshevism'. At the same time, and perhaps decisively, Schleicher was becoming increasingly disillusioned with Brüning; for although Hindenburg and Schleicher were not enamoured of coalition governments and desired 'strong' rule, they each hoped that such rule would nonetheless have some kind of popular mandate, which Brüning was manifestly unable to deliver. As a result Schleicher had become involved in a series of behind-the-scenes intrigues to try to obtain such a mandate by involving Hitler and other politicians in discussions aimed at getting some broad 'bourgeois' political front. Although these tortuous negotiations came to nothing in the short term, Brüning's difficulties in commanding support led Hindenburg to demand his resignation. On 30 May 1932 the Chancellor resigned, to be replaced by Franz von Papen, also a member of the Centre Party but one whose views were way to the right of its general political line.

Politics now took a decisively more reactionary course: Papen cut back on welfare payments quite dramatically, removed previous bans on the SA (the Nazi stormtroopers) and dissolved the Social-Democratic government in the state of Prussia. But although he was probably doing enough to satisfy most conservative circles (and Hindenburg was not keen to remove him from office), Papen, like his predecessor, now ran into problems with Schleicher on account of his inability to generate a broad popular mandate. Papen did not see eye to eye with Hitler, and his 'Cabinet of Barons' could rely on support from only the DNVP, DVP and BVP. The backstairs intrigue continued. Schleicher told Hindenburg that the army had lost confidence in the Chancellor and on 2 December 1932 Schleicher himself took over that position. In his attempts to find the kind of mandate his two predecessors had lacked, the new Chancellor embarked on a series of risky manoeuvres involving talks with trade-union leaders and those on the left wing of the Nazi Party. Needless to say, conservative circles were highly disturbed by these developments, as they were by Schleicher's apparent commitment to reflationary policies to counter the slump. This, and the fact that he too failed in his political intrigues to generate the broad support he needed, left Schleicher vulnerable to the same kind of manoeuvres he had himself practised for so long. Conservatives around Papen were finally able to come to a deal with Hitler offering firm right-wing government with a popular mandate (the large electoral support of the NSDAP), although, as Henry Turner has shown, it was touch and go as to whether agreement would be reached to appoint Hitler until the very last minute.

However, Hindenburg was finally prepared to countenance Hitler as Chancellor; and the latter was duly appointed to the position on 30 January 1933. At the time the Nazis were in a minority in the new cabinet; and older politicians such as Papen thought they would be able to control him.

The intrigues that brought Hitler into office rested on the fact that conservatives and Nazis shared many values – nationalism, anti-communism and a strong dislike of the Weimar Republic among them – and on their quite disastrous belief that they would be able to control and harness the Führer. Such collaboration is therefore not surprising. Perhaps more puzzling is that those who were to be the first political victims of the new regime, namely the Social Democrats and Communists, seemed to do so little to prevent the Nazi seizure of power. Generally the responsibility for this has been located in the tragic split between the SPD and the KPD and in the way the two parties spent so much time attacking each other. The Communists believed that capitalism had entered a final crisis, that fascism was a last-ditch effort to maintain the capitalist system and that proletarian revolution was now on the agenda. All that could prevent such a revolution, they believed, was the activity of Social Democrats in mislead-ing the German working class away from the revolutionary path. Thus, according to the Communists, the SPD had become a prop of capitalism and was denounced by the KPD as 'social-fascist'. There is no doubt that this attitude was suicidal and led to a gross under-estimation of the Nazi threat. Yet this is only part of the story.

First of all, it is not true to say that the KPD did not attack the Nazis: indeed, its members bore the brunt of the street fighting against the brownshirts. Second, the SPD also underestimated the fascist threat. Third, the leadership of the SPD itself was at least partly responsible for the split in the ranks of the German labour movement, as a result of its counter-revolutionary behaviour when in government immediately after the Great War, and also of the repressive policies adopted by Social Democratic police chiefs towards demonstrations of Communists and the unemployed, most notably on May Day 1929, when demonstrators in Berlin suffered fatalities at the hands of the police. Social Democratic city councillors were also often respon-sible for wage cuts and dismissals to balance budgets in the financial crisis of the depression; while nationally the SPD offered no alternative to the deflationary policies of Brüning or Papen.

However, the inability of the SPD and KPD to reach agree-ment resulted not only from the political divisions at leadership level. It was also a consequence of the social and economic fragmentation of the German working class in the wake of mass and long-term unemployment. Increasingly the SPD was a party of older, employed, respectable workers, while the KPD was overwhelmingly one of younger, unemployed workers who often lived in districts of high criminality. Unemployment set the unemployed against the employed, younger against older worker, men against women, region against region and factory against factory in the competition for jobs. Those with jobs were afraid of losing them; those without were incapable of strike action and as time passed sank into an ever deeper passivity. Unlike 1920, when the Kapp Putsch had been defeated by a general strike, the depression offered no such possibility with over 6 million Germans unemployed. Even if the German labour movement had been united, however, it is still most unlikely that it could have resisted the Nazi seizure of power with any degree of success, for labour stood isolated not only against the Nazis but against the rest of German society. In any case it would have been no match for the army. There is also considerable evidence that the experience of unemployment was so devastating for many workers, especially for the long-term unemployed, that it was more likely to result in apathy and resignation than in radical action.

At the end of January 1933 Hitler was appointed Chancellor in a coalition cabinet which contained only three Nazis and a majority of Conservatives and Nationalists, who thought they would be able to control him. The Social Democrats hoped that Hitler's period of office would be short-lived and that the next elections would unseat him. Both sets of hopes were to prove tragically mistaken.

3

The Nazi state and society

When President Hindenburg appointed Hitler Chancellor on
30 January 1933 there were only two other Nazis, Hermann Göring
and Wilhelm Frick, in the cabinet. That the Nazis were able to consolidate their power so quickly in the months that followed was in part
a consequence of Hitler's position as both Chancellor and leader of
the Reich's largest party. With Hindenburg's support he could rule
through emergency decree. The position of Göring, as Prussian
Minister of the Interior, was also crucial, for he used his power in
Germany's largest and most important state to control police appoint-
ments and put an end to any police action against the SA, the SS or the
nationalist paramilitary organisation, the Stahlhelm. In fact these three
organisations were co-opted into police operations on 22 February
1933 and were responsible for the beating and detention of large
numbers of Social Democrats and Communists, as well as Jews. The
position of Hitler was further enhanced by the fact that the Nazis
first took action against the German left, against Communists and
Social Democrats, which was often welcomed by and bred a false
sense of security among the middle-class parties, which were virulently
anti-socialist.

In February 1933 Hitler persuaded his conservative colleagues to
agree to the calling of fresh elections with the promise that this
would be the last time that Germans would be asked to vote for a

long time. Emergency decrees banned hostile newspapers and political meetings, even before fire destroyed the Reichstag building on 27 February. Few historians now believe that the Nazis themselves had organised the conflagration, but they certainly exploited the event, drawing up an emergency decree suspending freedom of the press, of speech and of association. Personal rights and freedoms had effectively disappeared and the auxiliary police (consisting, essentially, of SA, SS and Stahlhelm men), which Göring had created, was deployed against the Nazis' political opponents. Astonishingly, despite the atmosphere of terror and intimidation and the virtual impossibility of the KPD and SPD mounting anything resembling their usual election campaigns, the NSDAP still failed to win a majority of the popular vote, despite a significant increase in turnout. In these elections, held on 5 March 1933, the Catholic Centre Party increased its vote from 4.2 to 4.4. million, the SPD vote did drop, but by relatively little, and although the KPD, which had borne the brunt of Nazi attacks, lost over 1 million votes, it still won the support of over 4.8 million Germans. Hitler and his party won just under 44 per cent of the total vote, still not a clear majority, but enough to enable him to form a majority in the Reichstag in alliance with the DNVP, which polled 8 per cent of the total votes cast. On 23 March 1933 this majority was used to bring in the so-called Enabling Act, by which Hitler's government could rule without the need for action to be authorised either by the Reichstag or by presidential decree.

Coincident with these 'constitutional' changes at the political centre, in the localities the Nazi Party, sometimes on its own initiative, sometimes with official backing, had embarked upon a campaign of violence against its political opponents. Thus the seizure of power was far from peaceful. At the local level Nazis interfered in administration and the course of justice, as well as commercial life. In Brunswick their revenge was especially bitter: KPD and SPD buildings were raided, assets seized and party members beaten up. In some places temporary prisons or 'wild' concentration camps were set up by the SS, the SA and the police, as in the Vulkan docks in the north German port of Stettin and the Columbia cinema in Berlin, where, as early as March and April 1933, tens of thousands of Communists and Social Democrats were detained and some were tortured and murdered. Although some civil servants thought this state of affairs was temporary (a necessary prologue to normalisation), in fact it became permanent. This early violence, directed against the German left, was sadly not unpopular with many middle-class Germans but on the contrary seems to have met with some degree of approval.

The combination of central government initiatives and local activism also put an end to the powers of the various *Länder* (the states, e.g. Prussia and Bavaria) within Germany, which remained federal in structure until 1933. On 9 March Epp carried out a coup in Munich, turning out the former administration and replacing it with Nazi Party members. Reich police commissars, appointed by Frick, also removed the old authorities in Baden, Württemberg and Saxony. Then, in the first week of April, Reich governors took charge in every German state: all 18 of these were Nazis, most of them Gauleiter. The process of the subordination of the *Länder* to central government was finally completed by legislation which came into effect on 30 January 1934.

Other steps were taken to consolidate Nazi control of state and society. The civil service was purged of political opponents and Jews (with the exception, on Hindenburg's insistence, of those Jews who had served in the Great War). Independent pressure groups and political parties were dissolved or declared illegal. The trade unions were dissolved on 2 May 1933 and their assets seized. In June the SPD was banned. The various middle-class parties, generally in agreement with the violence directed against the left but also intimidated by it, offered no resistance and dissolved themselves in June; the Catholic Centre Party followed suit in July. (The KPD, needless to say, had already been illegal for some time.) Thus by the middle of 1933 and within six months of Hitler becoming Chancellor, Germany was a one-party state. The churches continued to enjoy a degree of organisational independence but in this they were almost unique. The only institution to remain untouched – for the time being – was the army. Hitler was aware that interference here might provoke a serious and possibly fatal challenge to his regime, especially while Hindenburg was still alive, and hence he sought to win military loyalty (not that difficult, given many of his aims) rather than to engage the generals in a struggle for power.

The consolidation of Nazi power rested on a mixture of centrally directed constitutional change and outright violence in the localities. Much of that violence was the work of the Nazis' organisation of storm troopers, the SA, under its leader Ernst Röhm. At the same time, however, personal and organisational rivalries within the Nazi movement generated hostility towards Röhm and the SA, as, for example, in the case of the SS and its leader Heinrich Himmler.

And the existence within the SA of some radical ideas about social change, some kind of 'second revolution', caused further disquiet. Most crucially of all, the army became increasingly worried by what it regarded as the SA's attempt to usurp its role and authority. The result, and one which stood Hitler in good stead with both the elites and the German public at large, was the so-called 'Night of the Long Knives' on 30 June 1934, when the Gestapo and the SS arrested and shot the leadership of the SA. Thereafter Hitler's position was practically impregnable. After Hindenburg's death on 2 August 1934 the army swore an oath of personal allegiance to Hitler, as did the civil service.

The Nazi state which emerged from these developments was one which would brook no opposition and which sought not only to repress and destroy all alternatives but to mobilise the minds of the people behind the Führer through active propaganda. The media were taken over by the agencies of Joseph Goebbels' Ministry of Propaganda, which further organised the mass rallies and public celebrations of the Third Reich. The syllabuses of the schools and universities were transformed to reproduce the crude racist and geo-political views of the Nazi leadership. Works by those of different persuasions were banned and burnt. The civil service, as we have seen, was purged of dissident elements, while previously independent pressure groups were taken over by the NSDAP. In place of the unions the German Labour Front (DAF) was created under the leadership of Robert Ley. In theory this was meant to be an organisation which reconciled the previously conflicting interests of workers and employers. In practice, although it occasionally caused problems for some employers, it became a mechanism for controlling labour (strikes were illegal in the Third Reich). Certainly it did not function as a trade union, for it played no part in the determination of wage rates. Nazi organisations penetrated private as well as public life. To refuse to allow one's children to join the Hitler Youth or the League of German Maidens could be dangerous; while various sporting and leisure activities were organised through the 'Strength through Joy' (*Kraft durch Freude*) movement. Veterans' organisations, cycling and tennis clubs, even gardeners' associations were encompassed by this process of co-ordination; and independently organised *social* life virtually disappeared.

The dissolution of independent organisations standing between the individual citizen and the state is of the utmost importance in understanding the apparent quiescence of the German people between 1933

41

and 1945. Even in liberal, pluralist societies the ability of individuals to stand up for themselves often depends on their ability to join together and gain institutional support from pressure groups (trade unions, professional associations). The destruction of independent organisations in the Third Reich, a one-party and terroristic state, as we will see, simply obliterated the necessary framework for action. In this context it is therefore not surprising that the most overt forms of resistance to Nazi government came from the army and the churches: that is, from places where dissidence could still possess some institutional backbone. This also explains the widespread privatisation of daily life in the Third Reich (much against Nazi wishes), the retreat from the public and political arena that has been recorded by so many oral historians. The difficulty of dissent was additionally compounded by the fact that the Nazi system rested upon what can legitimately be described as institutionalised terror.

In the Third Reich civil liberties ceased to exist. There was no recourse to the Nazified courts against the actions of the NSDAP, the SA, the SS, the Labour Service or the Wehrmacht. The slightest show of dissent was likely to be met with a beating, with arrest and imprisonment or with incarceration in a concentration camp. The first such camp was erected at Dachau just north of Munich as early as 22 March 1933 in a disused powder mill. Its first inmates were Communists and Social Democrats. As time passed, however, and especially from 1936, Germany's concentration camps took in ever more social groups deemed by the Nazis to be 'undesirable': anti-social elements ('asocials'), the 'work-shy', freemasons, members of small religious sects, gays and most notoriously the ethnic minorities of gypsies and Jews. A special concentration camp for juveniles was also opened at Moringen in 1940. The concentration camps played a crucial role in the escalating persecution of 'community aliens' (*Gemeinschaftsfremde*): those individuals regarded by the Nazis as a social, ideological or biological threat. The number of camp inmates increased dramatically: from 3,500 in 1935 to over 25,000 in November 1938. By this time only 20 per cent of those incarcerated in Buchenwald were political prisoners, whereas 75 per cent were 'work-shy' or 'habitual criminals'. After the pogrom of 9 November 1938 the first large-scale transfer of the 'racial enemies' of the Nazi state into the camps began. Under the control of the SS, these camps became part of a system of (in)justice that ran parallel to but completely outside the control of the police and the judiciary, i.e. 'outside' the law. Large numbers were taken into 'protective custody' and put in Dachau, Buchenwald, Sachsenhausen, Flossenburg and Mauthausen without any legal process. The Third Reich repressed its potential enemies with comprehensive and systematic brutality. At the same time the legal process itself became increasingly vicious: between 1933 and 1939, 12,000 Germans were convicted of high treason. During the war a further 15,000 were condemned to death. The treatment of Communists was especially brutal: of just over 300,000 KPD members in January 1933, over half were imprisoned or sent to concentration camps, while no fewer than 30,000 were murdered by the Nazis in the following 12 years.

The Third Reich witnessed what Ian Kershaw has described as the 'subjugation of legality'. There were large numbers of arbitrary interventions in the legal process. The amalgamation of the police with Himmler's SS guaranteed a further erosion of legal process, while many actions which lacked legal foundation, such as the execution of the SA leadership in 1934, were justified only retrospectively. In 1936–37 the SS began to round up 'habitual criminals' and 'asocials', not because they had broken any law but because of what they were in the Nazi mind: 'diseased', 'unhealthy', part of a problem of racial hygiene as well as criminality. (Many Nazis also tended to equate 'asocials' with some amorphous threat of social revolution.) Increasing numbers of state prisoners were handed over to the concentration camps and some were executed. On 7 September 1939 Himmler ordered a prisoner on remand to be handed over to the SS and shot. Hitler himself intervened to 'correct' what he saw as lenient court decisions, too. By October 1940 at least 30 Germans and many more Poles had been handed over to the SS and shot in this way.

It is not the intention here to claim that Hitler's position in the Nazi state rested exclusively on terror and intimidation: as we will see later, many aspects of policy enjoyed real popular support. But any attempt to assess the relationship between people and government in the Third Reich which ignores the oppression documented above clearly will not be satisfactory. That oppression was successful not only because of its comprehensive and even 'anticipatory' nature – people could be arrested *before* they had done anything – but also because it was based on a systematic and ubiquitous surveillance of the population. The Nazis, and Hitler in particular, were obsessed with public opinion. Hence the massive information-gathering activities of the Secret State Police (Gestapo). In every block of flats 'block leaders' reported on the views of the residents, on every factory floor stewards had a similar role. Most insidious of all was the way in which spying could even intrude into the family, as portrayed brilliantly by one of the scenes in Bertolt Brecht's *Furcht und Elend des Dritten Reichs (Fear and Misery of the Third Reich)*. Children indoctrinated in the Hitler Youth or the League of German Maidens could and did report the views of their parents to Nazi officials, who became an alternative source of authority to the parent, priest or schoolteacher. Indeed, some witnesses have memories of the period as one in which family ties were disrupted and generation set against generation. Thus those harbouring dissident opinions in Nazi Germany lived in fear of denunciation, which was often exploited by neighbours, former work mates, or even school kids who disliked their Latin master, to settle old and often personal rather than political scores. (In fact the success of surveillance was entirely dependent upon public willingness to denounce fellow citizens, albeit more usually for personal rather than ideological reasons, for there were relatively few Gestapo officers, as Robert Gellateley and Klaus-Michael Mallmann have demonstrated.) Deprived of civil liberties, Germans had no independent organisations to represent them; and they faced imprisonment or incarceration in concentration camps should their dissent take any public form.

In such a manifestly dictatorial state and one in which the *Führerprinzip* (leadership principle) was meant to be embodied, it might seem logical to imagine that government and administration functioned easily: Hitler, the Führer, gave the orders, and these were then transmitted downwards and enacted by the relevant authorities. There is no doubt that when Hitler wanted something he got his way. This was the case with the Sterilisation Law of 1933, which he pushed through against opposition within the Cabinet, and of the commitment to develop the *Autobahnen*, taken against the wishes of the railway lobby. Equally, some of the most momentous decisions made in the Third Reich, especially in foreign policy and military matters, were made by Hitler and no-one else. He was behind the decisions to reoccupy the Rhineland in 1936, *Anschluss* with Austria in 1938 and the invasion of both Czechoslovakia and Poland in the following year. However, there is now a body of research which suggests that the processes of German decision-making between 1933 and 1945, especially with regard to domestic policy, were much more complicated and in some cases even chaotic. In the first place, when the Nazis came to power they did not fuse the institutions of the Party and the state administration, in contradistinction to what largely happened in Russia after the Bolshevik Revolution. Thus there existed side by side institutions of the old bureaucracy and of the

NSDAP. As far as foreign policy was concerned, for example, the Foreign Office (under the direction of the conservative Konstantin von Neurath until 1938) faced competition from the Party's Joachim von Ribbentrop, who offered personal advice to the Führer. In the localities the agencies of regional administration often found themselves at odds with the party's powerful Gauleiter, whose access to the person of Hitler going back to the early days of the Nazi movement gave them considerable authority. The dualism of party and state apparatus was not the end of complexity in the government and administration of the Third Reich, however. In economic policy there was competition, especially relating to manpower and materials, between the Ministry of Economics, the Wehrmacht, the Gauleiter and, increasingly, Göring's Office of the Four Year Plan, which built up a massive organisational empire employing over 1,000 officials. This office, established on Hitler's instruction in 1936, typified one aspect of the Führer's style of rule, namely his frequent creation of institutions independent of both the NSDAP and the state bureaucracy to fulfil specific tasks but whose power often then expanded mightily. In addition to Göring's Office of the Four Year Plan there existed the Todt Organisation, subsequently taken over by Albert Speer, to deal with public works and later with armaments, the Hitler Youth under the leadership of Baldur von Schirach, and most infamously the hugely powerful empire of the SS, which took over responsibility for the concentration camps and subsequently the police, under the direction of Heinrich Himmler and Reinhard Heydrich. Initiatives from any particular central institution also had to confront and were often constrained or thwarted by the powers of the Gauleiter. In many ways these various bodies came to resemble personal fiefdoms owing allegiance only to the Führer, their powers circumscribed by no set of rules. During the war and with the conquest of Eastern Europe after 1939 these fiefdoms competed for the spoils of domination and their leaders are perhaps best described as competing 'warlords'.

It is crucial to realise that the different organs of party, state and the *ad hoc* bodies described above did not stand in any hierarchical relationship to one another: there was no rational, bureaucratic chain of command, nor were areas of responsibility clearly defined or demarcated. All certainly owed allegiance to Hitler, as head of state, party leader or their patron and creator, but for the most part they followed their own ambitions and interests. Thus decision-making in the Third Reich often began in an uncoordinated way and was not the simple result of directives from a central administration, though it is true that all the organisations claimed to be working towards the same goals as the Führer and would never have frustrated his wishes. This strange fragmentation of policy formulation and implementation was also evident in the conduct of the Reich Chancellery. Hitler had little interest in formal cabinet meetings of ministers and the number of such meetings declined from 72 in 1933 to only six in 1937 and just one in the following year. As a consequence policy could not be formulated as the result of regular or formal discussion between Hitler and his assembled ministers. The only figure who provided contact for the ministers with one another and between the various ministries and the Führer was the Head of the Chancellery, Hans-Heinrich Lammers. He received draft legislation from the ministries and presented it to Hitler for authorisation. The system – or rather the absence of anything resembling a system – thus had a hugely paradoxical consequence. On the one hand the Führer was all-powerful, the only source of real authority and linchpin of the government, yet on the other he was rarely involved in the day-to-day discussions which led to the formulation of policy. How could such a strange situation have come about?

A possible explanation and one that has been suggested by several historians is a highly 'intentionalist' one: Hitler designed the overt competition between the various agencies of state and party in order to strengthen his own unique position, in order to 'divide and rule'. There can be no doubt that the ability to play off state bureaucrats against Gauleiter, or Göring against Himmler, did give Hitler exceptional power, as we have seen already. It would also be odd if a person as astute and opportunistic as Hitler had not realised the advantages that accrued from such a set of informal and unregulated arrangements. However, more satisfactory explanations of the emergence of 'polycratic' decision-making can be found elsewhere, namely in the nature of the Nazi assumption of power, the structure of the Nazi Party and the charismatic roots of Hitler's position as Führer within both the NSDAP and the German Reich. Unlike the Bolsheviks in Russia, the Nazis in Germany did not come to power by overthrowing the old elites in a revolutionary upheaval but rather in collusion with them. Thus Hitler had to tread warily, at least in the early days of the regime, in his dealings with big business and in particular with the military establishment. Both of these groups exerted considerable influence, although the period between 1934 and 1937 did see a steady increase in the power and influence of those closest to the Führer (Göring, Himmler, the Gauleiter) in the party and a diminution in the authority of those, such as the state bureaucrats, who were more distant. In 1938 there was a decisive breach with the old order, as we will see.

A second cause of the complexity of power relationships within Germany after 1933 related to the nature of the NSDAP itself. The Party had been created for the sole purpose of propaganda and the winning of elections. It did not possess the organisational structure or ability to administer a modern state. Hence the continued existence of the former bureaucratic organs of state. Perhaps even more significantly, the NSDAP's total and devoted commitment to its Führer, the sole source of authority and an authority based upon his personal charisma, not upon a hierarchically determined or functional role, prevented the development of any bureaucratic-rational definitions of authority below the position of the leader. Thus the Nazi Party already possessed that potential for rivalry and competition for Hitler's support before the seizure of power which became even more marked in the Third Reich itself. The subsequent erosion of legality, the appearance of the Nazi warlords, the competition of leading figures in the regime were all consequences of the unique position of Hitler himself, the Führer unbounded by constitutional niceties or bureau-cratic rules. The behaviour and personality of Hitler thus became a major determinant of the style and indeed content of government after 1933. Initially Hitler performed as Chancellor in the way that the elderly and punctilious Hindenburg expected of him: he turned up in office hours to discharge his duties. After the General's death in August 1934, however, things changed quite dramatically. Hitler would stay in bed until late morning, read the newspapers in leisurely fashion, might meet up with Lammers and some senior members of the Nazi Party, but would then go off alone for a ride in his limousine. In fact he spent a great deal of time at his retreat in Berchtesgarten – in Bavaria and away from the Berlin he detested. One consequence of this has already been described: the piecemeal formulation of policy from 'below', from various agencies that coexisted and competed in the Third Reich. A second was that it was sometimes extremely difficult to get a decision out of Hitler: issues were often shelved for a considerable period, as occurred during the economic crisis of 1935–6, when a serious shortage of raw materials and foodstuffs arose. Hitler was especially loath to intervene where decisions might make him unpopular with the general public; and his retention of massive personal popularity throughout most of the regime's existence reflected this fact.

The absence of clear lines of authority, as well as Hitler's own behaviour, thus left a space in which personal conflicts and institutional rivalries flourished. As each organisation sought to outdo the other in its commitment to the Führer and his aims (even if no specific instructions were received from above), so a process took place, which Hans Mommsen has described as 'cumulative radicalisation'. Power relationships within the Third Reich were never static and the Nazis were never simply content to repress the opposition. The regime possessed an in-built dynamism that led to a significant realignment of forces to the detriment of the old elites but to the benefit of Hitler and the various bodies he had created. In late 1937 the Foreign Office under Neurath and sections of the army, including Werner Fritsch, its leader, and the Minister of War, Blomberg, voiced concern about Hitler's foreign policy aims, fearing they would precipitate a war. Shortly thereafter, in January/February 1938, it transpired that Blomberg had married a prostitute and an old rumour concerning Fritsch's homosexual past began to circulate again, and Hitler took the chance to act. The ensuing crisis had not been engineered by Hitler, as his initial shock made clear. However, he exploited the affair to bring about a significant shift of forces within the governmental apparatus. A large number of generals was dismissed or pensioned off; the new army leader, Brauchtisch, promised greater co-operation with the Nazis; a new chief of the armed forces, Keitel, was appointed; the position of War Minister was scrapped; and Hitler personally became commander-in-chief of the armed forces. Similar changes took place elsewhere: in the Foreign Office Ribbentrop took over from Neurath and new ambassadors were put in post, while the Ministry of Economics was also rendered more malleable. These various developments saw an increase in power of those close to Hitler and constituted a real blow to traditional conservative forces. They also gave rise to a radicalisation of Nazi policy in foreign affairs (the Austrian and Sudeten crises), economic preparations for war, which were already leading to serious difficulties as far as manpower, raw materials and capital were concerned, and an escalation of violence against Jews and their property, culminating in the *Reichskristallnacht* of the night of 9–10 November 1938, when synagogues were burnt down, Jewish shops plundered and about 30,000 male Jews dragged off to concentration camps. The evolution of Nazi anti-semitic policy and its dreadful consequences are discussed at greater length in the next chapter; suffice it to say here that the excesses of 9–10 November 1938 were followed by the centralisation of policy towards the Jews in the hands of the SS.

★   ★   ★

In these various ways there can be no doubt that the Nazis brought about a revolution in the nature of the state and German politics between 1933 and 1945. A much more difficult question is whether or not they also transformed the nature of German *society* in the same period, whether or not Hitler engineered a 'social revolution', to use David Schoenbaum's phrase. The NSDAP certainly claimed to be creating a new kind of society, a *Volksgemeinschaft* (a 'people's community'), in which the divisions that had previously rent the German nation asunder, divisions, for example, of class and religious confession, would be overcome and Germans would unite in common purpose behind their leader. This would be a racial but classless community. Whether the Nazis ever achieved this end and certainly whether they were successful in eradicating class and other identities is far from easy to answer and depends in part on what is meant by the terms 'classless society' or 'social revolution'. The remainder of this chapter explores the question of social change and revolution in the Third Reich. It asks if there was a revolution in property ownership or the distribution of wealth, i.e. if anything resembling what Marxists might recognise as a revolution actually took place between 1933 and 1945, and concludes with a resounding 'no'. However, that is not the end of the matter. There were other ways in which society was altered profoundly, in terms of social mobility, (possibly) gender and (arguably) modernity. Above all it was transformed by the politics of *race*. The extent to which mentalities were transformed and identities destroyed is also investigated below. Put another way, did Germans accept the idea of the *Volksgemeinschaft* in their heads and their hearts, and abandon traditional allegiances?

If we look at property ownership in the Third Reich there was no fundamental redistribution, despite the radical aspects of the early Nazi Party programme and promises to small businessmen and shopkeepers. In fact, Hitler, who had never been that enamoured of the more radical social demands of the Nazi left (in the SA and around Gregor Strasser), was already calming middle-class fears in 1928, making it clear that it was only *Jewish* property which would be expropriated. By 1933 most of the Nazi radicals had left the party, while the 'Night of the Long Knives' had destroyed the SA leadership in 1934. Ambitious projects on the part of Robert Ley, leader of the DAF, to expand its role and that of labour, were quickly crushed in the early days of the regime. In May 1933 those appointed 'Trustees of Labour' were recruited mainly from the ranks of business. In November of the same year the Labour Front's role was further restricted and its leadership purged; and in the following January the Law for the Regulation of National Labour replaced the previously elected 'factory steward' (*Betriebsrat*) with a new representative (*Vertrauensrat*) with a reduced role. The outcome of the elections for this new post was so disastrous for the Nazi candidates that elections were never repeated. In the Third Reich workers remained workers (at least before the massive importation of foreign slave labour during the war). Large landowners remained large landowners and the giant industrial trusts enjoyed huge profits as the major beneficiaries of the economic growth of the armaments boom of 1936–38. What property was confiscated was Jewish (or, after 1939, that of foreign nationals); and it found its way not into the hands of the small businessman, shopkeeper or peasant farmer but into the personal empires of the likes of Himmler and Göring. In fact, capital became more, not less, concentrated in the Third Reich. This did not mean, of course, that the relationship between big business and the state was always an easy one. In return for the destruction of the trade unions and the profits that accrued from lucrative armaments contracts, big business dared not risk non-compliance, for the state controlled imports, the distribution of raw materials, and wage and price levels. It also found itself in competition with the massive industrial empire that Göring had built up through his Office of the Four Year Plan and which received priority treatment in the allocation of raw materials. Yet industrialists were not expropriated, their property remained in private hands and some, especially those associated with the giant chemical company IG Farben, benefited enormously from Nazi rule. Profits rose faster than wages, rising by over 36 per cent between 1933 and 1939, while the share of wages in gross national income declined from 57 per cent in 1932 to just over 52 per cent in 1939, indicating a redistribution of wealth *away* from the working class.

Of course, this does not mean that internal class structures remained static; and there was a whole series of developments in Germany between 1933 and 1945, which arguably weakened class solidarity on the part of German workers. The terror, the repression of the SPD, the KPD and the trade unions, together with the arrest of large numbers of labour activists, made cross-community and inter-factory solidarities increasingly difficult to sustain. The rationalisation of industrial production in some plants has also been seen as weakening the role of skilled labour, traditionally the backbone of protest (though it is easy to exaggerate the extent of such rationalisation). The provision of welfare and medical support at the level of the individual factory increasingly tied the worker to his place of employment, in addition to Nazi legislation. The abandonment of collective wage agreements in favour of individual reward for performance removed yet another prop of collective action; while the deployment of over 7 million foreign workers during the war placed many German workers at the top of a racial hierarchy of labour and in supervisory functions. Whether this led at the level of the subjective consciousness of German workers to the destruction of class identity, however, is far from clear. This issue will be discussed at greater length in a later section of this chapter.

Despite Nazi promises to the German *Mittelstand* before 1933, capital continued to become more concentrated after the Nazi seizure of power. In general, larger firms were more successful in the competition for labour and raw materials than smaller ones; indeed, the number of independent artisans declined from 1.65 million in 1936 to just 1.5 million three years later. Equally the regime prevented radical attempts to destroy existing department stores, the competitive bane of small shopkeepers. This does not mean, however, that nothing at all was done for artisans and shopkeepers. Special taxes were levied on the large stores and it became illegal to erect new ones, while several consumer co-operatives were closed down and restrictions placed on door-to-door sales. Self-employed artisans now needed to be members of resurrected guilds and to possess certificates of qualification. They also benefited from the increased orders associated with the economic recovery of 1936–38. That more was not done for small business, however, and that its economic decline was relatively severe was less a consequence of deliberate Nazi policies than of the logic of industrial production. The great military power that Hitler wished to create could not be built upon small-scale and relatively inefficient producers, especially where raw materials and manpower were in short supply. It has also been argued that industrial and technological modernisation was not simply an instrumental necessity for military victory but that such modernisation was in fact one of Hitler's goals from the very start. This issue will be discussed at greater length below.

The fate of agriculture under the Nazis was not dissimilar. In Nazi ideology the peasantry was portrayed as the backbone of a healthy Germanic society, one uncorrupted by the evils of urban living. The

51

regime did alleviate some of the farmers' problems (although until 1935 hand-outs were more likely to go to the larger and medium-sized estates than to smallholdings), while the control of imports and an initial setting of agricultural prices at higher levels than in the depression offered further relief. However, government control of prices could prove a double-edged sword and came to be resented by the peasants. In addition farmers could not compete with industrial firms for labour as the gap between agricultural and urban incomes grew, especially in the arms boom of 1936–38. A further consequence was that Germany became more and not less urban between 1933 and 1945, as people deserted the countryside to earn higher wages in the towns. The explanation can once again be found not in ideology but in economic reality: the shortage of manpower in the boom years 1936–38, and even more so during the war, pushed up wage levels, even under the Nazi controls. By 1939 real hourly wages had risen by 7 per cent above the level of 1932 and real weekly wages by 23 per cent (primarily a consequence of a longer working day/ week). It is not surprising, therefore, that between 1933 and 1938 the number of German agricultural workers declined by 16 per cent (some half a million people). Contemporaries spoke of a 'flight from the land'. Whereas the Reich's agricultural self-efficiency increased only modestly (from 80 per cent to 83 per cent) between 1936 and 1939, agricultural imports increased by 50 per cent in the same period. The long-term processes of urbanisation and industrialisation were not halted by the Nazis, though it should be noted that these developments were no more dramatic than in many other European societies.

The economic experience of labour in the Third Reich was not one of greater equality. We have already seen that the share of national income taken by wages fell during the Third Reich. Without unions and with strikes being illegal, the class position could change little, for the DAF was not allowed any scope in the setting of wage levels. Within the working class, differences in earnings grew, as national and regional wage rates were abolished and payment was made solely according to the 'performance principle' (*Leistungsprinzip*) on an individual basis. This does not mean, however, that workers simply suffered under Nazism. Payment by results benefited healthy young workers, especially those with a skill, at the expense of the older and less productive. There is general agreement that between 1936 and 1938 the real value of take-home pay grew, although most of this gain can be attributed to the fact that the length of the working day increased rather than to an increase in real hourly wages. The 'Strength through Joy' organisation also provided some groups of workers with decent leisure facilities and holidays for the first time. The number of those enjoying KdF holidays grew from 2.3 million in 1934 to over 10 million only four years later. However, it was mainly white-collar and better-placed manual workers who were the prime beneficiaries. Only 15 per cent of the beneficiaries of KdF holidays were in fact manual workers (i.e. about 1 per cent of the German working class as a whole). What is more, while the 'Strength through Joy' organisation catered for the new mass tourism, upper-class holidaymakers continued to meet their recreational needs through the private travel agencies. Class was thus not banished from the holiday scene. Many workers also complained that the KdF gave special treatment to SA and SS men. Overall, the relationship between capital and labour remained fundamentally unaltered between 1933 and 1945: firms stayed in private hands, bosses remained bosses and workers remained workers. There were ways in which the working class was restructured, especially during the war, as already mentioned, and we will return to these in our later discussion of modernisation in the Third Reich.

That Marxists would recognise no 'social revolution' in the Third Reich, given the manifest and increasing inequalities in wealth and property ownership, is thus not surprising; but it should be remembered that the Third Reich only existed for six peacetime years and only 12 years in all. Furthermore, if we move away from class to other dimensions of social structure, the Third Reich may appear far less unchanging. Deep inroads were made, for example, into traditional patterns of social mobility in German society. Although it is true that most businessmen, diplomats, senior civil servants, academics and university students continued to be recruited from a very restricted social elite, new avenues of social advancement, of increased social mobility, did become evident, especially as a result of membership of the NSDAP itself. The proliferation of government and party agencies gave some degree of status and influence to Nazis of relatively humble provenance, even at the very centre of political decision-making. Being a Nazi, not an aristocrat or member of the educated middle class, was what secured advancement. In 1935 some 25,000 Germans got salaries from the party. Thereafter the expansion of the German Labour Front, the Nazi welfare organisation (NSV) and other offices became a ladder of mobility for hundreds of thousands of Germans. In fact, far more than in the Revolution of 1918, the old elites saw their power and influence dramatically reduced in the Third Reich. Whereas 61 per cent of army generals had come from aristocratic families in 1921, the figure had dropped to 25 per cent by 1936, though this process had begun before 1933. During the Second World War, of 166 German infantry generals no fewer than 140 were of middle-class origin. The aftermath of the July bomb plot of 1944 saw 5,000 'conspirators' executed, many of them from the great military Junker families (Stauffenberg, Moltke). Mobility – both social and geographical – was further extended by the evacuations and bombings of wartime, which threw people from different backgrounds and regions together, and by the racial reordering of society, of which much more will be said later. The employment of over 7 million foreign workers in Germany by 1944 also transformed the lot of 'racially superior' German workers, who now found themselves in supervisory positions over the foreigners.

This increase in mobility chances was not universal and it was not functional: for life chances were forged in the crucible of increasing economic inequality, racial discrimination, to which we will return, and political correctness. Nazis did well but Communists and Social Democrats suffered. Jews, gypsies, 'asocials', the hereditary ill, alcoholics, mental patients and gays did not enjoy the benefits of the 'Thousand Year Reich'. For them Nazi rule meant the barbarism of concentration and death camps. The Nazi paradise, even in its visionary form, was a paradise for some but not for others. What it meant for women is far from clear. The role of women in Nazi society sheds interesting light on the play between ideology and economic reality in Nazi Germany. It is well known that National Socialist theory proclaimed that the woman's role was in the home: to breed for the Fatherland and care for the husband/soldier. Thus the regime embarked upon a series of measures designed to encourage women to leave the factories, to marry and to reproduce. Abortion was prohibited; birth-control clinics were closed; access to contraceptives was restricted; incentives were given to encourage Germans to marry and have children, while greater welfare was also provided for mothers. However, this pro-natalist policy did not apply to Jews, nor to those deemed to be 'asocials', hereditarily ill or chronically alcoholic. Women in these categories were subject to a programme of compulsory sterilisation; and over 400,000 Germans (men as well as women) suffered as a result. In consequence Gisela Bock sees women as prime 'victims' of the Nazi era. If they were healthy and Aryan, the Nazi regime deprived them of control over their bodies by forbidding contraception and abortion. If they were 'unhealthy' or 'non-Aryan' they were forcibly sterilised. Furthermore, the idea that women belonged primarily in the home entailed discrimination against females in the labour market and explains why the industrial mobilisation of the female labour force in Germany lagged behind that of some other countries, even during the serious labour shortage of the war years. Yet ideological purity still had to give some ground to economic necessity: in 1933 almost 5 million women were in paid employment outside the home, whereas the figure had risen to 7.14 million by 1939. Labour shortage and rising wages thus drew many females into industrial employment, despite the regime's ideological goals. However, the rise in the number of women working outside the home scarcely outstripped the overall growth of the arms economy; and increased industrial employment in this period was matched by an increase in the number of women in that most traditional employment: domestic service. It was not until 1942 that the full mobilisation of female potential for the war effort was finally countenanced by the Nazi regime.

Bock's view that women were victims of the Third Reich is not shared by all historians. Claudia Koonz, for example, sees women as complicit in programmes to breed for the Fatherland and rear Germany's soldiers. Many young girls even experienced the League of German Maidens as a liberating experience, in so far as it took them away from parental controls, as Dagmar Reese has shown. Women may have been excluded from centres of power in the Third Reich; but they did join and play a role in Nazi women's and welfare organisations in their hundreds of thousands. Some were involved in the medical, welfare and nursing professions, which administered and often drove forward the campaigns of sterilisation, euthanasia and extermination. Many were perpetrators, just as many were victims; and many welcomed the return to 'traditional family values'. We need to banish the idea of a single female fate under Nazism and replace it with one that is nuanced by class, profession, region, religious beliefs, health and ethnicity.

A discussion of social mobility and the role of women leads to another set of questions about social change in the Third Reich, namely those generated by a discussion of 'modernisation'. Despite the agrarian and anti-urban rhetoric, the Nazis presided over a regime which saw increasing levels of industrial growth, urbanisation and female employment outside the home. The percentage of university students who were female grew (from 17 per cent in 1933 to

40 per cent in 1940). The percentage of doctors who were women also rose (from 6 per cent in 1930 to 8 per cent in 1939). These developments, together with increased social mobility and the destruction of the power of the traditional elites, are held by some to have constituted a 'modernisation' of German society. Such was argued strongly by Ralf Dahrendorf and David Schönbaum in the 1960s, though the former thought many of these processes were unintended by the Nazis and were either a result of long-term historical trends or a function of the changes necessitated by rearmament and the war economy. Recently some German historians have gone even further and portrayed Hitler as a conscious moderniser. Rainer Zitelmann sees Hitler as a lover of aeroplanes and motor cars, the builder of *Autobahns*, an advocate of mass consumption (the 'people's radio' and the 'people's car' – the VW), a proto-typical 'social engineer' and a supporter of a classless society, which rewarded individual effort rather than status and social background.

For Zitelmann even the conquest of *Lebensraum* in the east is to be explained in terms of the need for sources of raw materials and food, precisely because Germany itself would be in Hitler's vision a modern industrial state and a consumerist society. Michael Prinz stresses the Labour Front's modernisation programme, which incorporated the introduction of modern technology, the growth of functional rather than status elites, a rationalisation of labour processes, payment by individual performance and a welfare programme likened to the proposals of Beveridge in the United Kingdom! The mass tourism of the 'Strength through Joy' organisation and the production of mass consumer goods are viewed by Prinz as decidedly modern. So are a supposedly 'Keynesian' economic strategy, which removed unemployment, and attempts at biological social engineering – eugenics, after all, is a modern science. In the work of Götz Aly, Susanne Heim and Karl-Heinz Roth, even the 'Final Solution' of the Jewish question, involving cost-benefit analysis, bureaucratic detachment, the elimination of morality from calculation, and mechanised killing becomes a function of economic planning. That modernity facilitated but did not cause the Holocaust is also the more modest claim of Zygmut Bauer. It is certainly true that scientists and academics from many disciplines participated in or took advantage of Nazi territorial expansion in the east and its murderous consequences. Racial policy and resettlement programmes were aided and abetted by economists, statisticians, geographers, biologists, chemists, agronomists, social scientists and physicians. Some played this role because they could see no further than the laboratory and their own experiments. They regarded themselves as 'apolitical'. Others were intent on maximising their career chances and motivated by opportunism and personal gain, while yet others agreed with the ideological premises and politics of Nazism.

Scientific research did not die in Germany as a result of Nazi rule; and in some areas it took on breathtakingly original contours, as in the fight against cigarette-smoking (until the financial consequences of tax-loss became more important) and cancer. The regime taught females to inspect their own breasts. It encouraged Germans to eat healthily; and in areas of ante-natal and post-natal care significant strides were taken.

Yet the motivation of pro-natalism had as much to do with political/military as with welfare considerations. What is more, it was crossed and frustrated by racial imperatives. 'Ballast existences', 'useless eaters', i.e. asocials, habitual criminals, those with hereditary diseases, Slavs, gypsies and Jews were excluded from the provisions of welfare and care and subjected to a 'murderous science' of persecution, sterilisation and extermination.

The gaps in this project of supposed modernity are all too evident. Increases in female employment often took place against, rather than because of, Nazi intentions and can largely be explained by the state of the labour market, especially during the war. The plans of the German Labour Front were never realised; and in fact Hitler often had a hand in their frustration, as Robert Smelser's biography of Ley makes clear. If we look at the nature of the Nazi economy and its performance, things were also less clear cut than is argued by the theorists of modernisation. A popular image exists that Hitler's government solved Germany's most pressing economic difficulty – mass and long-term unemployment – and ushered in a period of growth and prosperity. While it is true that unemployment did disappear (albeit only with the armaments boom of 1936–38), that real wages increased in the same period (although primarily because people worked longer hours) and that a clear revival of industrial production took place, this is not the whole story. First, the German economy was beginning to show signs of recovery in the second half of 1932 and much of the recovery in 1933 can be put down to programmes initiated by earlier Chancellors. Second, the fundamentals of Nazi economic policy were not breathtakingly original. Budgets were not too unbalanced, high tax levels were maintained, savings encouraged and the prime goal of reducing unemployment was not allowed to engender inflationary processes, of which Hitler had a great fear (no Keynes here!). Third, most of the Führer's economic policies were not part of a coherent, long-term plan. Rather, as Harold James has written, they were 'provisional *ad hoc* measures' until war led to the conquest of new territories. Fourth, the apparently rapid solution of the problem of unemployment was based less on the creation of real new jobs than on various measures which took people out of the labour market without placing them on the unemployment register. Married women were actively discouraged from seeking jobs and many in employment were dismissed (scarcely modern!). State marriage loans encouraged single women to leave their employment; while those – men and women – purged from the civil service in 1933 were not allowed to register as unemployed. Many of the young unemployed males (some 240,000 in 1934) were drafted into the Reich Labour Service, while the reintroduction of military conscription in 1935 removed even more of them from the job market. In none of this is there a hint of a strategy of modernisation.

It is also true, as Nazi propaganda never ceased to stress, that the regime embarked on a series of job-creation measures, most famously in construction and road building (the creation of the *Autobahnen*). The sum of 5.26 billion RM was invested in such activities between 1933 and 1935. Yet even here one must be cautious: a smaller sum was invested in road building in 1934 than in 1927; and until 1935 the same could be said of investment levels in housing and transport. (The explanation is that local authorities rather than the central state had been responsible for much of such activity during the Weimar years, a fact that has often been overlooked by many impressed with Nazi economic performance.) Recovery was not equally rapid across all sectors: only in 1935 did levels of employment in the building industry reach those of 1928. Similarly the production of machine tools overtook the output of 1928 only in 1935.

Jobs were created first through the proliferation of the number of public officials administering the civil service and the various Nazi party agencies, and second by increased arms expenditure, although much of this was disguised in the form of work-creation schemes in the early years of the Third Reich. Between 1933 and 1935, 5.2 per cent of German GNP was devoted to rearmament – twice the amount spent on work-creation schemes. The boom of 1936–38 was in every sense of the phrase an 'armaments boom', which did much to remove the problem of unemployment but nothing to modernise the German economy or cure its structural defects. By

1939 the economy was suffering from a shortage of skilled man-power, materials and capital. Consumer goods had recovered and manufacturers increased production by lowering the quality of their products, not by technological innovation. Many of the savings for investment were created by artificial exchange rates, price controls and restricting the share of national income taken by wages. The German economy only became a truly modern, technologically inten-sive economy after 1945. This also gives the lie to the argument that industrial production was so rationalised in the Third Reich as to lead to a complete restructuring of the labour force. In any case, slave labour was far from rational in many of its dimensions and scarcely 'modern'. For, as Harold James and Richard Overy point out, per capita productivity rose relatively little across the German economy in these years, especially in comparison with other industrial economies. Mass consumption, a new consumerism, also remained an unrealised dream. No worker ever had a Volkswagen, though some got radios. Workers were not the main beneficiaries of KdF programmes, as we have already seen; and those who did not fit the character of 'healthy Aryan' were excluded from whatever economic goods were available. This was not an open consumerist society.

The inequalities of wealth, property ownership and life chances that continued to exist in Nazi Germany make it difficult to speak of any kind of fundamental change in social structure; and increased social mobility was open only to those who fulfilled political and racial criteria. But that is not the end of the matter. For the war did produce profound social changes. As already noted, the great increase in geo-graphical mobility as a result of evacuation and bombing, together with enormous labour shortage, did loosen older solidarities and create new – though not necessarily welcome – job opportunities. This was a form of scarcely intended modernity – the modernity of mass destruction. The employment of millions of foreign labourers placed German workers in supervisory functions and structured the working class along racial lines, to some extent dissolving older solidarities. Even here, however, there were contradictions. Ulrich Herbert's brilliant study of foreign labour in the Third Reich reports on the way in which there was a constant tension between the racial ideology of the regime and the realisation that foreign labourers per-formed best when they could receive certain rewards and became integrated into the labour force. The latter realisation was enforced by the war and was not a consequence of any modernising ideology. On the contrary, it was often subverted by or came into conflict with economically dysfunctional racial imperatives. A similar point can be made about the concentration camps and their increasing contribution to the German economy from 1942, when they were incorporated in armaments production. Whereas previously work in the camps had constituted a form of punishment and torture, the work of the inmates was increasingly rented out by private companies; and it became the case in the camps on German soil that skilled inmates were less likely to be worked to death than those who worked in construction. In the east, however, all categories of inmate were worked to death and economic considerations played second fiddle to the racial imperatives of Nazi ideology. The ideological goals of Nazism entailed violence and barbarism for the dissident, the 'unhealthy' and the 'non-Aryan'. Whether one chooses to call such goals 'modern' or not, surely misses the point. What was important about Auschwitz was not electric fences and a modern technology of slaughter but the slaughter itself.

The Nazis did not remove the inequalities that underlay class; but in one regard they did fundamentally transform German society. That society was restructured according to *race*. Until recently, discussions of Nazi racial policy concentrated upon the extermination of Jews and − to a lesser extent − gypsies. It has become increasingly clear, however, that the project of 'racial hygiene' entailed far more than this. All those that the Nazis considered 'unhealthy' were to be removed from the 'People's Community' of pure Aryans. Thus it was not only Jews and gypsies who were refused maternity and child benefits, post-natal care, welfare support and 'Winter Support' but also those Germans the Nazis deemed to be political opponents, the 'hereditarily ill', 'asocials' and 'habitual criminals'. In 1936–37 large numbers of vagrants, the homeless, prostitutes, casual workers, 'asocials', 'habitual criminals' and homosexuals were rounded up and sent to the concentration camps, not because of what they had done but because of what they were − because they were deemed by the regime be of no 'biological value'. Racial and social hygiene fused in the minds not only of the Nazis but of many in the social work and medical professions; and it manifested itself in a variety of obscenely unpleasant ways. In June 1933 marriage loans were refused in cases where one of the prospective partners had a 'hereditary mental or physical illness'. The Sterilisation Law of 14 July 1933 allowed the compulsory sterilisation of the 'hereditarily ill', i.e. of those deemed to be (in Nazi terms) congenitally feeble-minded, schizophrenics, manic depressives, those who suffered from Huntington's chorea, hereditary blindness or deafness, chronic alcoholics and those with serious physical deformities. On 24 November 1933 permission was given to castrate 'dangerous habitual criminals'; and in fact biological tests were carried out on all prisoners in the Third Reich. Between January 1934 and September 1939 some 320,000 Germans were forcibly sterilised. From June 1935 abortion was made compulsory for women up to and including six months of pregnancy when 'health courts' deemed the women in question to be 'hereditarily ill'. (The involvement of health professionals in all of these processes should be noted.)

Racial criteria also determined the treatment of workers after the importation of millions of foreign labourers during the war. German workers found themselves in supervisory positions; in terms of pay, Western foreign workers (French, Dutch, Italian) were treated more like German workers, though deductions from their wages were greater and they were forced to live in camps; whereas Poles and Russians received much lower remuneration, were subject to a great deal of physical abuse and were regulated by special legislative restrictions, though some of these were on occasion relaxed for reasons of productive efficiency. Sexual relations with Germans on the part of Poles and Russians were punishable by death.

A classic example of the barbarous consequences of the racial hygiene project was provided by the 'euthanasia' programme: the murder of mentally handicapped Germans. Though it began with Hitler's response to a specific request, described in the next chapter, the 'euthanasia' programme was thought out and administered by leading psychiatrists, doctors and administrative experts. Beginning with children, it came to incorporate adults in June or July 1939. Although the opposition of leading figures in the Catholic church led to the campaign's suspension, it resumed (though now under the cloak of secrecy) under the circumstances of war and witnessed the shooting of large numbers of mental patients in Polish hospitals. Some 70,000 Germans were put to death in this programme.

The most infamous aspect of the Third Reich was also the consequence of Nazi racism: the slaughter of gypsies and Jews. Whether or not genocide was intended by the Nazis and Hitler from the very start is the subject of heated debate and will be discussed in the next chapter. The exclusion of gypsies and Jews from a 'healthy' Aryan nation, however, began long before 1939. With the approach of the 1936 Olympic Games in Berlin as an excuse, hundreds of gypsies were removed to a 'resting place' at Marzahn, a site next to the

Berlin rubbish tip. It was soon enclosed by barbed wire and became a de facto concentration camp, whence gypsies were sent to the gas chambers of occupied Eastern Europe in 1942–43. Better known, of course, is the fate of the Jews and that fate is recounted in the next chapter.

★   ★   ★

That Nazi society underwent significant change as a result of racial policy is indisputable. The life chances of its citizens depended more upon their race and 'racial purity' than on any other single fact. In other regards far less changed. Despite greater social mobility, the objective bases of class society (gross inequalities in income and property ownership) remained. In this sense the Third Reich was in 'objective terms' a class society. However, it is possible to argue that the Nazis did succeed in creating their *Volksgemeinschaft* in subjective terms, that the Germans did unite behind Hitler and that the traditional divisions and loyalties of class, religious confession and region were overcome. Thus Nazi ideology and propaganda successfully papered over real economic and social cracks. Such, at least, is what the Nazis themselves claimed. It is a claim repeated by David Schoenbaum, among others. The idea that the Nazis were successful in this regard obviously implies a change in the values and beliefs of millions of Germans. However, it is here that the problems begin. Just how do we know what 'Germans' were thinking and feeling between 1933 and 1945? In this context one simply cannot ignore the terroristic nature of the Nazi state and its ubiquitous surveillance of the population, nor the fact that the Ministry of Propaganda under Goebbels controlled all forms of public expression. Without unions or independent pressure groups to represent them, Germans who dared overtly to criticise the regime faced the threat of prison, concentration camp, violence at the hands of the SA, the SS and the Gestapo, and even death. Under such circumstances it is highly misleading to construe the relative absence of overt opposition or resistance (and in fact there was far more of both than is often imagined) as tacit acceptance of or agreement with the aims of party and government in the Third Reich.

The pressures against dissent were reinforced by two other factors. When the Nazis came to power in 1933 approximately 6 million Germans were without work. Despite the inducements that led many women to leave the factories and thus opened up jobs for men, despite the reintroduction of military conscription and the creation of the Labour Service, in which six months' service was compulsory for young adult males, and despite the 'massaging' of the unemployment statistics (an activity scarcely unique to the Nazis), there were still 2 million jobless at the beginning of 1936. Only in the subsequent boom was unemployment eradicated. This level of unemployment could be manipulated by the state and the NSDAP: opponents of the regime did not find it easy to find a job, while those in the Hitler Youth or the Nazi Party received preferential treatment. This was one of the factors that led to such a massive expansion in the size of the two organisations after January 1933. At that point the Hitler Youth had a mere 55,000 members, yet by the end of the same year almost half of German youth aged between 10 and 14 years had joined the organisation and over 4 million were members by the end of 1935. The NSDAP witnessed similar expansion, increasing its membership by 200 per cent between January 1933 and the end of 1934. By 1939 it had no fewer than 5 million members. Obviously there could be many reasons for this rush to join, but there is no doubt that, for many, job prospects and opportunism were the driving forces. The second factor that reinforced the hold of the Nazis on German society was the advent of the Second World War in 1939. To resist government in time of war could be construed not simply as opposition to particular policies but as treason; and in any case the terroristic nature of the regime became even more marked during the conflict. The number of crimes which warranted the death sentence was now increased from three to 46; and over 15,000 such sentences were meted out by the courts of Germany during the war.

Given this, it is scarcely surprising that historians of resistance and opposition in the Third Reich traditionally concentrated their attention on a small number of identifiable resisters, most commonly in the shape of the military. The disquiet of Generals Beck and Halder in the late 1930s and, above all, the July Bomb Plot of 1944 have formed the foci of attention. The story has also been told of the activities of the 'White Rose' group of Munich students during the war, the double role of German counter-intelligence (the *Abwehr*) under Admiral Canaris and the opposition of the 'Red Orchestra' of communist and left-wing artists and intellectuals. Yet this account of resistance has been substantially modified by recent research. First, it turns out that many of the military bomb plotters of 1944 did not necessarily share democratic values and that some were racist. It has also been observed that by far the largest number of Germans incarcerated (in either gaol or concentration camp) for political crimes came from the working class. Third, the conceptualisation of attitudes in Nazi Germany as either 'resistance' on the one hand or 'consent' on the other misses that broad spectrum of opinion which ran from positive acclamation, through consent, acquiescence and indifference, to dissent, opposition and outright resistance. Where most people stood on this spectrum is far from clear, given the repressive nature of the regime.

This is not to claim that the Third Reich was based exclusively on repression. A range of policies met with approval from large sections of German society. It does mean, however, that any reconstruction of what ordinary men and women thought of their Nazi rulers is far from easy and that silence must not simply be construed as acceptance. The relationship between the government and the German people needs to be analysed from the standpoint of specific groups and demands careful, differentiated examination. In attempting such an analysis we are aided by two relatively unusual sources: the intelligence reports of the Gestapo and those of the SPD in exile (the so-called SOPADE reports). Both sets of reports are sufficiently nuanced to carry some degree of conviction. Even more remarkably, given their totally different origins, they are often quite similar in their conclusions concerning the state of popular opinion between 1933 and 1945.

An analysis of the relationship between the army and government in the Third Reich demonstrates several traits that could be found in other groups and institutions in the same period. First, there was a whole series of policies with which the High Command could identify more or less totally. These included the attack on Communists and Social Democrats, the stress on traditional family and moral values, the destruction of divisive Weimar politics, increased military expenditure, rearmament, the reintroduction of conscription and the restoration of national greatness through the undermining of the provisions of the Treaty of Versailles. These reflected the values that the Nazis shared not only with the Wehrmacht but also with the German middle class at large. Tensions between Hitler and the army became more evident, however, when he interfered in military matters or when leading generals, such as Ludwig Beck, came to fear that his foreign policy would lead to defeat, as it did in 1936 in the case of the remilitarisation of the Rhineland, two years later in the case of the *Anschluss* with Austria and again in the Sudeten crisis. (This stance had little to do with a principled or moral opposition to Nazi policy but is probably best construed as military self-interest.) In any case Beck's plans fell to pieces when Britain and France appeased Hitler over Czechoslovakia and strengthened the position and prestige of the Führer. Much of the origins of opposition to Hitler within the army during the war stemmed from similar motives: resentment at Hitler's meddling in military matters and the fear that such meddling would lead to defeat. However, there also emerged within the army what might be described as a more moral and principled opposition, which became disgusted by the barbarism of Nazi rule. This opposition, which included Moltke and Stauffenberg, had contacts with like-minded elements within the churches and even with some socialists. It played a major role in the attempt to blow up Hitler in 1944, though again it should be noted that many of those involved in the plot were not necessarily free of anti-semitic or undemocratic attitudes.

A similar mixture of institutional self-interest, agreement with certain aspects of Nazi policy and yet principled opposition was to be found in the German churches. The Evangelical (Lutheran) Church had a long tradition of obedience to political authority and had strong historical links with the conservative Prussian state. It detested socialism, identified with the Nazis' stress on traditional moral and family values, and in no way resented the passing of the sinful and materialistic Weimar Republic. It also gave full support to the restoration of national pride. Yet attitudes towards the regime and its policies within the Protestant Church were far from united. There were some, calling themselves 'German Christians', who gave full support to the system and who have been described as the 'SA of the Church'. They believed that Christianity was essentially a Nordic religion that had been corrupted by Jewish influences (more than a few problems here with the historical figure of Christ!), that Germans had a divine mission and that the 'Jewish Problem' had to be solved. Such strange creatures, however, were not typical of the Evangelical Church as a whole. On the one hand, the church hierarchy sought to avoid conflict with the regime without endorsing all aspects of its policies. On the other, and like the army, it became disquieted when Nazis of a more radical and pagan persuasion attempted to interfere in its internal affairs. There was also within the ranks of German Protestantism a principled opposition which denounced the brutality, godlessness and racism of Nazi rule and established the 'Confessing Church' (*Bekennende Kirche*), whose most famous representative was the pastor Dietrich Bonhoeffer, who became involved in active resistance to Hitler. Even in the case of Bonhoeffer, however, it has been noted that his concern for Jews who had converted to Christianity was significantly not replicated in the case of non-converts. Thus there was no one Protestant attitude towards government in the Third Reich but a mixture: acceptance of some policies but the rejection of others. It was most definitely not the case that Germans abandoned their churches – or at least not the older generation of Protestants and Catholic church-goers. In 1934, for example, when two Protestant bishops were arrested, there were angry demonstrations for their release.

The allegiance of the Catholic Church in Germany to Hitler and his regime was even more problematical, given its prior commitment to Rome, though the rapid signing of a Concordat between the Papacy and the Third Reich on 20 July 1933 eased relations. Again the Catholic Church could identify with Nazi attacks on Communists and Social Democrats. It supported the emphasis on traditional morality and shared much of the Nazi view of the role of women and the family in German society. It too had regarded the pluralist and divisive democracy of Weimar as less satisfactory than some form of corporate state, advocated in a papal encyclical of 1931. However, Nazi anticlerical campaigns in 1936–37 and 1941, interference with Catholic schools and youth organisations, and the harassment of its priests also generated institutional opposition to the government. In some cases opposition possessed a moral dimension, as it did most famously in the case of the policy of euthanasia. This was denounced from the pulpit by the Catholic Bishop of Münster, von Galen; and the regime was forced to abandon the open murder of the mentally and physically infirm, though the euthanasia campaign did continue in secret. (Significantly neither the Catholic nor the Evangelical Church took such a stance in the case of Nazi anti-semitism.) Some Catholic priests, such as Alfred Delp, also became involved in the resistance to Hitler that led to the bomb plot of July 1944. Once again a range of attitudes prevailed; and once again the Catholic community of Germany remained loyal to its church. The arrest of popular priests, attempts to remove crucifixes from school classrooms and other forms of Nazi interference were sometimes met with popular outcry in areas that were solidly Catholic. There were demonstrations, mothers refused to send their children to school and threats were made not to pay taxes. In such situations the local NSDAP was often forced to back down after instructions from the party hierarchy.

The army and the churches provided the most obvious examples of overt dissent and opposition in the Third Reich. This was no accident:

in both cases organisations with some limited degree of autonomy had continued to exist and thus could provide an institutional backbone and collective support for acts of dissidence. Hence their prominence. In the case of the German working class, on the other hand, the institutional framework for collective resistance had been utterly destroyed. Gone were the unions and those enormous political parties (the KPD and SPD) with their numerous ancillary educational and leisure organisations. It was also the German working class which, with the notable exception of the racial minorities, bore the brunt of Nazi violence and repression. By far the largest number of Germans arrested, imprisoned and incarcerated in concentration camps for acts of political opposition were workers. Both the KPD and the SPD continued their underground opposition to the regime throughout its existence and re-emerged after 1945, albeit temporarily in the case of the Communists. (Interestingly, it was not the Nazis but the Cold War which killed off the Communist Party, which still recorded the support of over 20 per cent of the electorate in some of the towns of the Ruhr in the British zone of occupation shortly after the war.) Of course, most workers did not become involved in the dangerous pursuit of active resistance, but a majority of labour historians concur that the government was never successful in winning the active support at least of the older generation of workers. Rather, these older workers retreated into private life, into sullen apathy and resignation.

From Gestapo reports and those of the SPD in exile it is clear that there was widespread discontent over food prices in 1935 and early 1936. There were even some strikes among those building the *Autobahnen* in 1935, in spite of the consequences of such illegal protest. The constraints against collective action, however, were sufficiently massive to make it extremely rate. On the other hand, there was an increase in acts of industrial indiscipline (slow working, absenteeism) in 1937–38, which worried the government sufficiently for it to criminalise such activity. It is probably wrong to characterise these developments as some form of political opposition, but they do indicate that workers were still aware of their position as *workers* – scarcely surprising – and had not swallowed the myth of the 'people's community'.

Even in the case of the German working class, however, this is far from the whole story. There were aspects of Nazi policy that could find a positive resonance even here. Although suspicious of the regime's motives, many workers did welcome the leisure activities

67

and holidays provided by the 'Strength through Joy' organisation. Those who secured jobs after earlier unemployment may well have felt some sense of gratitude to their new rulers. The beneficiaries of payment by results and those who achieved supervisory functions (especially during the war with massive labour shortage and the employment of foreign slave labour) also had some reason to feel not too aggrieved. In this context the age factor probably came into play. It is fairly clear that older workers who had belonged to the communist and social-democratic movements were in the main not persuaded by the Nazi message. Conversely, younger workers without such a background, arguably the beneficiaries of the 'performance principle', were generally reckoned to have a more positive image of Nazism. It was through Germany's youth that Nazi ideology and organisation made inroads, for example, into rural communities.

That youth was more susceptible to Hitler's appeal than older generations with class and confessional loyalties seems beyond dispute. The Munich students of the White Rose resistance group in Munich were far from typical of their generation. Far more enjoyed their activities in the Hitler Youth or the League of German Maidens. Yet even here the Nazis did not have it all their own way. As the Hitler Youth became increasingly militarised and bureaucratic, and its leadership older, so it became less popular with German boys. The ability of the Nazis to influence the popular culture of younger Germans was also decidedly limited. The regime preached against the evils of swing music (American, decadent) and, even worse, jazz (decried as negroid), but this did not stop many middle-class adolescents listening to it. Admittedly the phenomenon of 'Swing Youth' cannot by any stretch of the imagination be described as dissident, but it is yet another indication of the fact that Germany's rulers could not simply rid the population of its likes and dislikes and impose their own tastes. This point applies even more forcefully to some sections of working-class youth in the large cities, where street gangs with intriguing names (the Navahos, the Raving Dudes – note the Hollywood rather than Germanic references) were formed. These *Edelweisspiraten* ('Edelweiss Pirates'), as they became known, rejected the values of the regime, sang popular American hits and parodied the anthems of the Hitler Youth. The actions and life-style of these gangs were regarded as sufficiently threatening by the Nazi authorities that over 700 gang members were rounded up in December 1942 and several of the leaders hanged. In Cologne in 1944 some gang members even teamed up with army deserters, escaped prisoners of war and foreign labourers in armed conflict with the forces of law and order.

Obviously the *Edelweisspiraten* were typical neither of German youth nor of the population at large, but we have already seen enough to realise that there was far from conformity of opinion within the Third Reich and that the population had not been 'brainwashed' into a simple identification with everything Nazi. In general, Nazi propaganda both before and after the seizure of power was most successful where it could play upon the traditional prejudices and values of German middle-class society, upon issues such as nationalism, anti-socialism and family values. Sadly it has to be admitted that the clearing of the streets of tramps, delinquents and gypsies also could count on a good deal of support from this quarter. Whether this also applied to anti-semitism is a much more contentious issue and will be debated in the next chapter. However, where the regime opposed traditional loyalties, it was far less successful, most obviously in the case of the churches, but also among the German working class.

Some aspects of the regime were more popular than others. Whereas the shortages of 1935–36 generated a great deal of grumbling, the relative economic prosperity of 1936–38 saw more positive attitudes towards the government. And although the Nazi Party and its self-seeking functionaries became increasingly detested, the personal popularity of Hitler reached unprecedented heights. One of the most important reasons for this, of course, was the foreign policy success that could be attributed to Hitler almost entirely. Yet even here popular opinion was far from one-dimensional. The remilitarisation of the Rhineland, *Anschluss* with Austria and the occupation of Czechoslovakia were popular with the German public not simply because they restored the country's national pride but also because they were won *without war*. All the evidence suggests that there was a widespread fear within Germany of a repetition of the events of 1914–18 and that the initial reaction to the invasion of Poland in early September 1939 was one of dismay. Thereafter, however, the rapid and relatively bloodless victories of 1939 and 1940, first in Poland and then in the west, brought Hitler to a pinnacle of personal power and popularity, though fears and anxieties again accompanied the invasion of Russia on 22 June 1941. Subsequent defeats and the intensification of the Allied bombing of German cities obviously led to a deterioration of morale and a loss of faith in the Führer; for that faith had always been predicated upon the most remarkable success. Charisma rarely survives defeat; though even here it has to be said that the front-line troops remained loyal to Hitler, as American interviews at the end of the war made clear.

Amid the conflicts, competition and rivalries of the Third Reich, the 'Hitler myth' constituted an integrative factor. Created first within the NSDAP itself, then communicated to the German people at large, mainly through the massive activities of Goebbels's Ministry of Propaganda, it fed above all off the foreign policy and military victories of 1936–42. It gathered momentum from the fact that Hitler represented a national unity and apparent harmony that had been so notoriously lacking in the days of the Weimar Republic. Additionally, Hitler was seen as a man of the people, one who did not put on the airs and graces assumed by Göring and who was above the corruption and self-interest that characterised so many in the Nazi Party between 1933 and 1945. Hitler was even regarded by many in German society as a representative of law and order! This image gained hugely from the destruction of the SA leadership in the 1934 'Night of the Long Knives' and seemed to confirm that the Führer was a moderate, in contrast to the thugs who were responsible for direct violence against people and property.

The Third Reich erected a system of repression and domination that became ever more radical in the implementation of its aims. During the Second World War it was revealed in its full and barbarous colours, as the few constitutional and legal constraints that had survived – and they were few indeed – were swept away in the nakedness of military occupation and genocide.

4

War and destruction

In the course of the Second World War the 'warlord' nature of the Nazi regime reached its apogee. This was not simply because Germany was now at war – and on the eastern front in a war of almost unprecedented barbarity – but also because in the newly occupied territories, especially Poland and the Soviet Union, government in the usual sense was replaced by the naked domination of Nazi warlords, who competed for the spoils of victory and controlled massive fiefdoms. Most notable of these was the SS empire erected by Heinrich Himmler. By 1944 there were 40,000 concentration camp guards, 100,000 police informers, 2.8 million policemen and 45,000 officers of the Gestapo. This expansion was a consequence both of increased repression within Germany during the war and of the extension of concentration camps and their role not only as prisons or institutions of slaughter but also as sources of slave labour. The armed units of the SS (the Waffen SS), which played a disproportionate part in the implementation of the politics of genocide, recruited a further 310,000 men from ethnic Germans outside the boundaries of the Reich. Other Nazi warlords included Fritz Sauckel, whose fiefdom dealt with the deployment of manpower, Robert Ley, who was in charge of housing, the chief of the German Labour Front, Fritz Todt and his successor Albert Speer, who had control of armaments and munitions, and Hermann Göring, whose Office of the Four Year Plan spread its empire over transport, mining, chemical production and price controls, and plundered occupied Poland. The proliferation and fragmentation of offices, which effectively prevented any co-ordinated economic and military strategy until the very last days of the war, was further compounded by the increased authority of the Gauleiter, whose direct links to Hitler subverted the influence of the state bureaucracy. In fact, as the war progressed, it was agencies of the party and the Führer's 'special authorities' which increased their power at the expense of career bureaucrats. The Gauleiter were entrusted with many new tasks relating to the war effort at home but also often put in charge of the newly occupied territories.

What gave the Gauleiter and the special agencies their authority was their personal contact with the Führer, whose power was now absolute. The erosion of traditional governmental structures, which permitted the unchecked exercise of such power, also took place at the very centre of the Reich. The role of Hans-Henrich Lammers of the Reich Chancellery was now undermined, especially after the invasion of the Soviet Union, by the rise of Martin Bormann as head of the Party Chancellery. It was now Bormann who controlled access to Hitler and often bypassed governmental bodies as far as legislation in the occupied territories was concerned. He also over-saw what information reached Hitler and transmitted the Führer's 'decisions', which often amounted to no more than casual remarks at the dinner table, to various agencies of the party and state for imple-mentation. The utterly informal nature of such decision-making was nowhere more obvious than in the euthanasia campaign.

The precise circumstances surrounding the start of the euthanasia programme are far from clear. It appears that a not insignificant number of Germans, with the rhetoric of Nazi eugenics in mind, had petitioned the KdF for permission to end the lives of their deformed and defective children. It was one such petition that set this barbarous campaign in motion, probably in 1939. A father peti-tioned Hitler for permission to have his badly deformed child 'put to sleep'. Hitler agreed and had his personal doctor carry out the task. In this way the process of euthanasia began, although the Führer's eugenic beliefs and commitment to racial purity obviously provided the underlying rationale for such action and there had been talk of such a programme for some time. Indeed, to agree with Ian Kershaw, here was another example of German citizens 'working towards the Führer', by requesting actions which they knew he supported. Hitler gave the Führer Chancellery the signal that similar cases could be dealt with in like fashion and subsequently that adults as well as children could be incorporated into the campaign. Chillingly the doctors of Germany's asylums co-operated in providing the Führer Chancellery with lists of names of the deformed and mentally ill. Ultimately 70,000 were murdered in a programme which was deliberately removed from the control of either the Ministry of the Interior or the health authorities. Some of those responsible for the euthanasia programme were subsequently involved in the extermination of Polish Jews. The inhumanity of the euthanasia programme typified not only the murderous nature of Nazi rule but also its total disregard for due process of law. No law was ever passed authorising it, no minister consulted about it. It began with a single case and no written authorisation. When Hitler was later called upon to issue some written authorisation, he put down a few lines on his own writing paper and – significantly – back-dated the authorisation to the first day of the war.

The onset of war also radicalised the Nazi persecution of 'outsiders' and their treatment in the concentration camps. Previously relatively few 'community aliens' had been killed. Now inmates were shot, given lethal injections, subjected to medical experiments, worked to death and transported to the gas chambers. In 1942 there was a further radicalisation: almost one-third of all 'asocials' incarcerated in the Mauthausen concentration camp died each month in the following year. At the same time there was an increase in the number of official executions in the Reich. Whereas 139 death sentences were passed by the German courts in 1939, the number rose to 4,000 in 1942 alone. In January 1945, 800 prisoners in the Sonnenberg penitentiary (a state prison, not a concentration camp) were executed by 85 officers. At the same time the massive increase in concentration camp inmates (over 700,000 by early 1945) went hand in hand with an increasing likelihood of death – in forced marches and as a result of forced labour, disease, and even gas chambers, which were used in Ravensbrück and Mauthausen.

Terrorism and racial violence culminated in the attempted extermination of gypsies and of European Jewry. The number of gypsies who died in Nazi death camps is not clear: calculations vary from 220,000 to over 1 million. Of course, the annihilation of Jews was on an even greater scale. We have already examined (Chapter 1) the violent anti-semitic prejudices Hitler expressed in *Mein Kampf*. Although the theme was played down in Nazi electoral propaganda between 1928 and 1933, it subsequently re-emerged with the most ghastly consequences. In the spring and summer of 1933 much of the violence of local Nazi Party branches and SA groups was directed at Jews and their property. In Berlin East European Jews from the capital's Scheunenviertel were seized and subjected to physical abuse by groups of Nazis. In Breslau Jewish lawyers and judges were assaulted. In Mannheim the local SA ordered the closure of Jewish shops. In Straubing Nazi excesses against local Jews ended in murder. Partly to control such uncoordinated violence, the regime organised a boycott of Jewish businesses for 1 April 1933, although this seems to have had little success with the German public at large. On 7 April 1933 the 'Law for the Restoration of the Professional Civil Service' expelled Jews from state employment (unless they or their fathers had served in the Great War – a concession to Hindenburg). Eighteen days later further legislation restricted the number of Jews who could be appointed to jobs in German schools or universities. In September 1933 Jews were forbidden to own farms or engage in agricultural employment and in the following month they were debarred from membership of the Journalists Association. Anti-semitic initiatives were both public and private, both centrally directed and local. Already in March 1933 the City of Cologne closed municipal sports facilities to Jews. In April Jewish boxers were expelled from the German Boxing Association.

Anti-semitic sentiment on the part of Nazi radicals and the SA intensified in 1935, not least as a kind of substitute for the loss of power and position resulting from the execution of their leaders in the Night of the Long Knives. Anti-Jewish violence escalated at the end of March and again in June. It was complemented by announcements from the Ministry of the Interior that further legislation, excluding Jews from the armed forces, would be forthcoming. So, rather like the boycott of shops in 1933, the promulgation of the 'Nuremberg Laws' on 15 September 1935 was a response to the undisciplined excesses in the lower ranks of the Nazi movement, as well as a further statement of the regime's prejudice. The Nuremberg laws drew a distinction between those of Aryan blood, who held full rights as 'citizens', and non-Aryan 'subjects'. The 'Law for the Defence of German Blood' prohibited marriage and sexual relations between Jews and non-Jews. Jewish families were henceforth forbidden to employ Aryan servants under the age of 45 and Jews were not allowed to hoist the German flag, which was now to be black, red and white with a swastika in its centre. The laws were expanded in various supplementary decrees later in the year, which forced the remaining (previously exempted) Jewish civil servants, teachers, doctors and lawyers in state employment out of their jobs and deprived Jews more generally of voting rights and civil liberties. The 'Law for the Protection of the Hereditary Health of the German People' of October 1935 also aimed to register members of 'alien races' and those of racially 'less valuable' groups. Germans now required licences stating that their prospective marriage partners were 'fit to marry'; and marriage to gypsies, negroes and their illegitimate offspring was forbidden. The aim of this legislation was to isolate Jews from the rest of German society and to make their lives so unbearable as to force them to emigrate. Indeed, this was to remain the dominant theme of anti-semitic policy until the outbreak of war in 1939.

A further wave of anti-Jewish activity was sparked off by Hitler's speech at the 1937 Nazi Party rally in Nuremberg, when he fulminated against 'Jewish Bolshevism'; while *Anschluss* with Austria in the following year produced a more blatant and sadistic display of anti-semitism in the newly annexed territory. Indeed, Austrians seemed 'more avid for anti-Jewish action' (Saul Friedländer) than the Germans of the Old Reich (Germany proper). In Austria the pressure to force Jews to emigrate became more systematic and some were physically pushed over the borders into Switzerland, Hungary and Czechoslovakia. Meanwhile further anti-semitic violence occurred in the spring and early summer of 1938 in Germany itself and was accompanied by various initiatives on the part of the regime. In April 1938 Jews were obliged to register their property. In June 10,000 'asocials' and 'habitual criminals' were arrested, of whom 1,500 were Jewish. The Jews among them were shipped off to Buchenwald concentration camp, which had been set up in the previous year. In July various financial services (real estate, stockbroking, credit information) were forbidden to Jews, as was medical practice. In September Jews were forbidden to practise law in Germany.

Though Hitler had called an end to spontaneous acts of violence in June 1938, fearful of their impact on public opinion and foreign governments, his reaction to the murder of a German diplomat in Paris at the hands of a Jewish assassin provides us with an interesting insight into his calculating but nonetheless vicious opportunism. After the assassination he specifically declared that the party was not to initiate anti-Jewish outbursts but also that it was not to prevent them. In effect this was to give the green light to Goebbels, who was to be the principal architect of the pogrom of *Reichskristallnacht* (Reich Crystal – on account of the broken glass – Night) of 9–10 November 1938, even though the pogrom was far from totally co-ordinated from the top. Jewish businesses and synagogues were attacked and burnt down by members of the SA, SS and NSDAP. Large numbers of Jews were assaulted and some murdered. In the aftermath some 10,000 Jews were taken into custody and authority for dealing with the 'Jewish Question' was transferred to the SS. The intention now was to speed up the deportation of Jews from the Reich, and Adolf Eichmann took charge of this process.

A host of measures sought to drive Germany's Jews out of public and social life. Immediately after the pogrom a decree effectively banned Jews from all economic life with effect from 1 January 1939. On 15 November 1938 Jewish children were expelled from the schools. Two days later, Jews were excluded from the welfare system and subsequently were deprived of access to public places, such as theatres, cinemas, concerts, museums, sports facilities. The aim of forced emigration was repeatedly re-stated; and the separation of Jews from the rest of German society continued apace. From 28 December, for example, Jews had to occupy homes housing only other Jews. In 1939 further decrees established that existing contracts with Jewish businesses could be rescinded and debarred Jews from all health-care activity (such as pharmacy and dentistry). The possibility of Jewish life in Germany was effectively destroyed.

The outbreak of war, which saw a radicalisation of all aspects of Nazi rule, was also accompanied by a radicalisation of policy towards the Jewish community. In fact Hitler had predicted such a development in a speech to the Reichstag on 30 January 1939, when he threatened that the advent of war would end with the annihilation of European Jewry. Other countries were already refusing to accept large numbers of Jewish emigrants, thus undermining Nazi strategy, even before 1939. The outbreak of hostilities made voluntary emigration virtually impossible. Furthermore, the acquisition of territories in the east brought ever more Jews into the rapidly expanding Reich. *Anschluss* and the annexation of Czechoslovakia placed 300,000 more Jews under Nazi control. The occupation of Poland added a further 3 million; and subsequently the number of Jews in German-controlled territory rose to 10 million. The strategy of emigration had thus become impossible. With the defeat of Poland, part of the country – the 'General Government' under Hans Franck – was transformed into a massive ghetto of 'inferior peoples', to which rounded-up Jews were transported in cattle wagons and where they were kept in the most unsanitary and increasingly enclosed conditions. An early result for many was death through disease and starvation, especially as forced labour became the norm in the Jewish ghettos. Yet this was nothing to what happened in the wake of the invasion of Russia in 1941. The war against Russia was, to use Hitler's own words, a 'war of extermination', in which the army co-operated with the security organisations in killing the political commissars attached to the Red Army. Himmler's right-hand SS-man, Heydrich, issued instructions that Communist Party officials and 'Jews in the service of the [Russian] state' should be liquidated. As more and more POWs and Jews fell into German hands, the *Einsatzgruppen*, the squads which implemented Heydrich's instructions, became increasingly indiscriminate in their campaign of murder. Now all Jews, not just adult males, fell victim to mass murder by shooting, in which not only the regular army and the SS were involved but also police battalions, which often included Lithuanians and other locals with strong anti-semitic traditions. Subsequently the order was given for the deportation of German Jews (*Aktion Reinhard*) to the east. Extermination camps, such as those at Belzec, Treblinka and Sobibor, were built; and former members of the euthanasia campaign became involved in preparations for the systematic murder of Jews by gassing (a 'solution' more 'humane' for the murderers in Himmler's opinion!). This 'Final Solution' was the Holocaust, the extermination of millions of Jews.

Given Hitler's vicious anti-semitic prejudices, what he had written in *Mein Kampf* and the content of his Reichstag speech of January 1939, it is not surprising that the 'Final Solution' has been seen as the logical and inevitable outcome of the Führer's intentions. There are several reasons, however, why I believe such a view to be too simple. First, many of the anti-semitic actions in the Third Reich were not necessarily initiated at the political centre, especially given the polycratic system of government and the institutional chaos described in the previous chapter. Second, it is far from clear that the 'Final Solution', as it occurred – that is the systematic extermination of Jews – was always the ultimate goal. These remarks will be explained in greater detail below; but I wish to make it clear at the outset that they are in no way intended to absolve Hitler from personal responsibility for genocide. Even where others within the Nazi Party were responsible for anti-semitic initiatives (Goebbels in the case of *Kristallnacht*, Göring in the case of the Aryanisation of the economy), they always acted with reference to the Führer's wishes and known views. It was, after all, Hitler's 1937 denunciation of 'Jewish Bolshevism' that formed the background to the events that led up to the *Reichskristallnacht*. Several of the most important decisions, such as the decision to deport German Jews to the east, required and got Hitler's approval. Any suggestion that Hitler did not know about or approve of the 'Final Solution' is simply not credible. Saul Friedländer has also made the interesting point that, whereas the Führer was intimately involved in the evolution of anti-semitic policy in the early days of the regime, his later role was one of issuing fairly general (albeit often murderous) policy statements, the implementation of which varied from one Gauleiter to another (as in the case of Germanisation in Poland).

This said, the actual development of Nazi policy towards the Jews was often a response to initiatives that had begun from below: the organisation of the 1933 boycott of Jewish businesses, for example, was partly an attempt to harness the violence to people and property dispensed by local Nazi groups. The same could be said of the enact-ment of the Nuremberg Laws in 1935. In a sense, spontaneous and often unpopular thuggery was replaced by more formal and cen-tralised, though equally repulsive and discriminatory, policy and legislation. Such was also the case after *Reichskristallnacht*, when responsibility for the Jews was transferred to the SS. Furthermore the vagaries of anti-semitic policy, what Schleunes has described as the 'twisted road to Auschwitz', make it far from certain that Hitler and the Nazis already had a distinct view as to how they would deal with the Jews. It is not clear that they always intended genocide. Indeed, there is considerable evidence to the contrary. Here we have to be careful not to read Hitler's early remarks with the hindsight of the Holocaust. Hitler did speak of ridding Europe of Jews and did on occasion use the language of 'eradication' (*Ausrottung*). In fact he used this term more frequently than the word for extermination (*Vernichtung*). Even in his infamous speech to the Reichstag on 30 January 1939, in which he spoke of the annihilation of the Jewish race in the event of war, Hitler also spoke of an alternative: 'The world has enough space for settlement'.

Until 1939 Nazi policy placed its faith in deportation and enforced emigration, i.e. a non-genocidal strategy. Walter Gross, head of the NSDAP's Racial Policy Office, reported what Hitler had told him about the aims of the Nuremberg laws, namely that they were intended to limit Jewish influence inside Germany and to separate Jews from German society. They were also enacted because 'more vigorous emigration' was necessary. Somewhat ironically, emigration to Palestine was especially promoted! Statements from the SD (Security Service) in May 1934, others at a conference in the Interior

78

Ministry in September 1936 and yet more in Goebbels' diaries in November 1937 all confirm that total emigration was the desired policy. This became even clearer after *Anschluss* in 1938, when 45,000 Jews were expelled from Austria within six months, as it did again after the subsequent occupation of the Sudetenland in Czechoslovakia, when vigorous attempts were made to expel Jews from the newly occupied area. On 12 November 1938 Heydrich reminded listeners that the priority of the regime's policy was to get Jews out of Germany. Less than a month later (on 6 December) Göring, following instructions from Hitler, again gave top priority to emigration; and in 1939 German representatives attended meetings of the Intergovernmental Committee for Refugees, which met at Evian, and discussed plans for Jewish emigration from Germany. In 1939, 78,000 Jews were forced out of Germany and a further 30,000 out of Bohemia and Moravia. The body created by the Nazis on 4 July 1939 to represent Germany's Jewish community also had one task above all else: to facilitate emigration. Most significantly of all, Jewish emigration was not forbidden by the Nazis until October 1941.

This strategy of enforced emigration proved unsuccessful when countries such as Switzerland, the United States and Britain began to limit the number of refugees they were prepared to accept. It was also overwhelmed, as we have seen, by the massive increase in the number of Jews in the expanded Reich after *Anschluss*, the annexation of Czechoslovakia and the conquest of Poland. However, the occupation of Poland opened up new and even more dreadful possibilities. Eastern Europe was to be restructured along racial lines. This involved the settlement of some areas in Poland by ethnic Germans, the uprooting of Poles to other areas of the country, the transportation of Polish Jews to ghettos in specified towns in Eastern Poland and ultimately their resettlement in a huge reservation to the south of Lublin. Between December 1939 and February 1940, 600,000 Polish Jews were transferred to this area in cattle trucks. The sheer numbers involved, however, soon made it clear that the strategy could not succeed, especially as Germanisation policies drove Poles into areas previously set aside for Jews and as Franck, the head of the General Government, complained that his administration could no longer sustain all the incomers on top of the 1.4 million Jews already under his jurisdiction. The policy of deportation was brought to a temporary halt. In the meantime the Jews in Poland were forbidden to change residence, subject to a curfew, obliged to perform labour services, forced to wear a yellow star and enclosed in ghettos.

Even as the plan for the Lublin reservation came to nothing, however, sections of the SD were working on the 'Madagascar Plan', a scheme to deport Jews to the island in the Indian Ocean! Such a scheme, a clear indication that the 'final solution' was not the only possibility, had been discussed as an alternative to emigration even before 1940 and the defeat of France. In fact it had first been suggested by the anti-semite Paul de Lagarde and was popular in right-wing circles in Germany in the 1920s. Heydrich had expressed an interest in a Madagascar project in 1938 and Himmler is known to have been enthusiastic. The idea was to transport 4 million West European Jews to the island, leaving Eastern European Jews in Poland as a deterrent to American intervention in the war. With the defeat of France, this plan seemed for a short period realistic and was taken quite seriously by Heydrich and some of his associates. Franck even instructed his staff to abandon further ghettoisation plans in Poland precisely because of Hitler's anticipated plans to send the Jews to Madagascar after the war! It has to be remembered that defeated France possessed Algeria, Morocco and Tunisia in this period. What is more, serious discussions were taking place in the Reich Chancellery at this time about the possibility of a German Central African Empire. In the summer of 1940 the names of possible governors of a future German East Africa were mentioned. It seems, at least according to Götz Aly, that Heydrich at this time preferred the Madagscar 'solution' to 'biological extermination', which he believed too 'undignified' a course of action for civilised Germans. Of course, this plan not only required the co-operation of Vichy France but also the defeat of enemy seapower. That Britain remained undefeated put an end to it.

In the early, euphoric weeks of the war against the Soviet Union the deportation of Jews to somewhere east of the Urals was still being contemplated; but the logic of a war of 'extermination', the barbarity of the German military effort (some 3 million Russian POWs were shot), increasing logistical difficulties and the slowdown in the advance of the German forces, who found ever more Jews under their control, led irreversibly to a massive escalation of murder. In this process it was not just the SS, Nazis and the *Einsatzgruppen* who played a part, but also the army itself. Yet, emphatically, none of this would have been possible without the obsessive anti-semitism and anti-Bolshevism of the Führer himself.

The development and scale of the killing in the Soviet Union initially varied from one area to another, which suggests there was no uniform project of total annihilation at this stage. However, although Heydrich's order to kill specifically referred to Jews in the service of the Russian state, the *Einsatzgruppen* often killed all Jewish males and in some cases also the Jewish women and children they encountered. The move to wholesale slaughter took place more quickly in some units than in others. In many cases, as in Lithuania, the killing was aided by local residents with strong anti-semitic traditions. By the winter of 1941–42 some 500,000 Jews had been shot. At the same time, with increased Russian resistance, the idea of resettlement across the Urals ceased to be feasible, while ever more Jews were forced into ghettos and the strain on German resources became ever greater. Locally SS leaders embarked upon the mass slaughter of Jews. Subsequently the gas chambers of the extermination camps became the instrument of that genocide, which has become known as the 'Final Solution'.

The point at which Hitler or other elements of the Nazi leadership decided upon the attempted extermination of *all* Jews is far from clear. I have already given my reasons for rejecting the view that this was always the intention of Hitler and his regime. However, it is also true that the mechanised slaughter of the death camps, unlike the first shootings of the Russian campaign, must have been the consequence of a policy decision. It could not have been 'improvised'. Thus even those such as Martin Broszat and Hans Mommsen, who see the evolution of anti-semitic policy as driven by deteriorating circumstances and cumulative radicalisation, rather than central policy, do recognise that some kind of central decision was necessary for the 'Final Solution'. So does Saul Friedländer in his subtle account of the interaction of intention and reaction to circumstance in the development of Hitler's ideas of a 'solution' to the Jewish 'problem'. When the decision to exterminate was taken is a source of heated debate. For Richard Breitmann the decision was made before the invasion of the Soviet Union, in April 1941. Most historians settle for a later date. Christopher Browning believes that the initial victories over Soviet forces now enabled the Nazis to do what had previously been unthinkable. So the fateful decision was taken in the summer of 1941 in the euphoria of victory. The Swiss historian Philippe Burrin, on the other hand, sees the decision as a consequence of the slowdown of Germany's advance and of increasing German difficulties, and pushes it back to a later date in 1941. The most recent research of Götz Aly on Nazi resettlement policy and the discoveries of Christian Gerlach, however, now suggest – and with great plausibility – that the decision was not taken until mid-December 1941. This conclusion is reached on the basis of entries in Goebbels' diary dated 12 December 1941 and in Himmler's official diary (*Dienstkalendar*) dated 18 December 1941. This would explain why the date of the Wannsee Conference had to be postponed and its agenda changed – from expediting deportation to the 'Final Solution' – to suit the new policy. At this point things were going seriously wrong in Russia with the rise of partisan warfare. At the same time the entry of the United States into the war removed the last reason for constraint; and the resettlement policy had broken down. On 5 December the German army had been halted at the gates of Moscow and temperatures on the Russian front had fallen dramatically. Zhukov had appeared on the scene with 100 divisions, of which the Germans had no prior inkling. In the Reich itself Cologne had suffered heavy bombing on 7 December, as had Aachen the following day. In these circumstances the solution of the 'Jewish problem' moved into its final, barbaric phase. Whether the Nazi Holocaust was simply pre-programmed by Hitler's anti-semitic beliefs or was the consequence of a more complicated process of 'cumulative radicalisation', driven forward by many different agencies and not only by the Führer, however, the indisputable result was the extermination of millions of Jews.

This raises a further question: to what extent was Nazi policy towards the Jews a consequence of popular anti-semitism? To what extent was it what 'the German people' wanted? For Daniel Goldhagen the answer is simple: 'Germans' favoured the Holocaust; and that is why it happened. He portrays German history as 'abnormal' in its eliminationist anti-semitism and recites examples of anti-Jewish hatred stretching back over centuries. In seeking to explain how millions of Jews could be shot in cold blood by 'ordinary Germans' who made up the police battalions, he finds his answer in the prevalence of murderous anti-semitic views. Now there can be no doubt that large parts of German society possessed some history of anti-semitism. James Retallack has identified a widespread conservative anti-semitism in Baden and Saxony in the middle of the nineteenth century, while Olaf Blaschke has analysed the growth of anti-semitism in Catholic rural areas. In both cases the issue of rural credit and a discourse of Jewish 'usury' played a part. Anti-semitic political parties had risen to prominence in the 1880s and 1890s. Though these declined after 1900, anti-semitism was deeply embedded in various conservative organisations, such as the Agrarian League (*Bund der Landwirte*) and the Pan-German League before the First World War, and in the DNVP thereafter. Indeed, Nationalists in Hitler's early cabinet played a part in the drafting of anti-semitic legislation. The Evangelical (Protestant) Church adopted the discriminatory 'Aryan Paragraph'; and although the Confessing Church of Dietrich Bonhoeffer did all it could to protect Jews who had converted to Christianity, it did little for Jews who had not. Neither Church openly denounced anti-semitic policy. The German professoriate colluded in ridding their profession of Jews; and university students were even more vicious in their hostility, embracing the Nazi position to a very large extent. The Catholic Church in Germany in general subscribed to what Saul Friedländer describes as 'moderate anti-semitism', wanting to remove 'undue Jewish influence' from social and cultural life. There is further evidence that the Nuremberg Laws were widely welcomed in 1935.

However, although the evidence of fairly widespread anti-semitism is indisputable, it does *not* justify Goldhagen's conclusion that the Holocaust was what most Germans wanted and that this made Germans in some way 'abnormal'. First, large numbers of non-Germans were implicated in the extermination of European Jewry: Latvians, Lithuanians, Ukrainians, Rumanians. Second, pogromic anti-semitism was more at home in Eastern than in Central Europe, for reasons that were discussed in the first chapter. The heartlands of anti-semitism were Poland, Rumania and the western parts of Russia. At the end of the First World War 250,000 Jews were massacred by Ukrainians, Russians and Poles. Third, the barbarism of Nazism extended not only to Jews but also to gypsies, to Slavs generally and even to those Germans it regarded as 'diseased' or 'alien'. Some 3 million Russian prisoners of war were shot by the German army. Arguably, therefore, genocide was informed not only or even necessarily by a specific anti-semitism but also by more universal conditions of inhumanity. Fourth, Goldhagen simply ignores a large amount of evidence that does not fit his schema. Christopher Browning has demonstrated how 'ordinary Germans' could kill Jews for reasons that had little to do with ideological anti-semitism (peer pressure, group solidarity, following orders); and yet he is able to come to this conclusion using much the same material as Goldhagen. Why the Nazis were so concerned to keep the 'Final Solution' secret is difficult to explain, if the German people wanted the Holocaust. Equally, the resort to gas chambers to reduce the impact of slaughter on the perpetrators would make little sense if Goldhagen's claims were true. In fact the German Jewish community was relatively well integrated into German society before 1914 and inter-marriage with Christians was far from uncommon. The largest party in the Reich at this time, the SPD, was not anti-semitic. Its leader, August Bebel, characterised anti-semitism as the 'socialism of fools'; many of the party's leaders were Jews; and when one of these, Paul Singer, died, 1 million German workers turned out for his funeral. The boycott of Jewish shops in 1933 was not popular, as Goebbels noted. Nazi injunctions not to trade with Jews were ignored by most peasants in the mid-1930s and by many in small towns in the late 1930s. Economic interest clearly outweighed prejudice here. Outright violence against Jews often produced an unfavourable reaction; and one of the reasons why the Nuremberg Laws were popular was that they were seen as bringing to an end the measures against the Jews, rather than as being a prologue to genocide. What this means, therefore, is not that Germans were not anti-semites but that we should beware of generalisations on this score. Moreover, popular anti-semitism was neither a prime concern of most Germans, nor was their anti-semitism usually eliminationist, except in the case of Nazi radicals and a few others. Goldhagen tends to lump together all forms of anti-semitism and assume their desire to exterminate Jews rather than to demonstrate it. In any case, even if the Holocaust were 'popular' – and we have seen enough to know that such a claim is unwarranted – it would still not explain the 'Final Solution'; for we have seen the tortuous way in which this policy was finally decided.

There is clearly an intimate connection between the war in the east and the 'Final Solution'. For Hitler the war, and in particular the war against Russia, was nothing less than a crusade: a crusade against the restrictions of Versailles, against Marxism and against the Jews, who, he believed, controlled Russia and international Marxism. Yet the development of German foreign policy between 1937 and 1941 was not simply the consequence of long-term ideological goals and it did involve the opportunistic exploitation of crises not necessarily of Hitler's own making. On 5 November 1937 Hitler had addressed Germany's military leaders in the context of growing economic difficulties (the navy, for example, was facing an acute shortage of raw materials) and a fear that any military advantage the country enjoyed at that moment might soon be eroded. Hitler stated that a war for living space could wait no longer than 1940 and that it would begin with Austria and Czechoslovakia. However, any opportunity that arose before that date might be exploited for the desired aims. Yet *Anschluss* with Austria was triggered when the Austrian Chancellor Schussnigg unexpectedly called a plebiscite on the issue of uniting with Hitler's Reich and subsequently when, in response, the German march into Linz received a hugely enthusiastic welcome from the locals. Equally, the precise timing of the invasion of Czechoslovakia was a response to Czech mobilisation in May 1938, and the invasion of Poland followed the refusal of Britain to accept German diplomatic initiatives. That Hitler acted opportunistically and that others were involved in the escalation of these various crises is beyond dispute. It is also true that military and economic pressures played a role additional to the demands of ideology. Yet this cannot justify the conclusion that Hitler had no long-term aims of expansion: he did, of course, and that is precisely why he used opportunities in the way he did to expand eastwards. In fact every extension of the front in the Second World War (outside the Pacific area) was the result of Nazi initiative (in Poland, the Netherlands, France, Norway, Russia), except in the case of Greece and Albania, where, aware of the potential threat to the Rumanian oilfields, Germany had to bail Mussolini out of his military difficulties. As early as 31 July 1940 Hitler was planning the destruction of Russia in a campaign that was supposed to last no more than five weeks. Once again a great deal of the motivation was diplomatic (the desire to bring Britain to surrender), military (fear of Soviet military expansion) and economic (the fear that such expansion might include the Rumanian oilfields), although the tortured argument that the invasion of the Soviet Union was a 'pre-emptive reaction' to a likely Soviet attack beggars belief. Again we can see that the Second World War was not simply a consequence of Hitler's ideological obsessions. But it was most definitely a result of these, too. Once it began, the anti-Jewish and anti–Bolshevik crusade unleashed the horrendous consequences of these obsessions.

The invasion of the Soviet Union in 1941 rested on a grossly mistaken view of Russia's resources and military capacity. It led, of course, to the defeat not only of the German armed forces but of everything that Hitler and his murderous regime stood for. El Alamein and Stalingrad spelled the beginning of the end; and Hitler could no longer escape the charge that his was the major responsibility for the disaster. Under these pressures Hitler's health deteriorated and with this deterioration came increased nervous anxiety and depression. He spent more and more time on his own and increasingly lost touch with reality, as he visited neither the front nor his German public. Physical illness and mental depression became even more serious in the aftermath of the July 1944 bomb plot; and the few who had access to the Führer spoke of one who had aged dramatically in the last years of the war. One result was that although Hitler's personal authority was never challenged by any other figure in the regime, it was an authority exercised in an increasingly arbitrary and infrequent manner: it became more difficult to get a decision out of him as the Reich fell apart. When Hitler did intervene in military matters, on the other hand, the benefits were, at best, somewhat dubious. He was not an ignoramus, as far as the waging of war was concerned, and he had a good memory for detail. However, he relied too much on his own experience as an infantryman in the First World War and failed to appreciate the need for fast rather than heavily armed tanks to combat the Russians. His preference for offensive rather than defensive weapons also led to vast expenditure on the V1 and V2 rockets and a failure to develop defensive rocketry that might have been deployed against the Allied bombing raids, which flattened so many of Germany's major cities. Here the concentration of power in Hitler's hands was clearly dysfunctional for the war effort. Yet the disaster, when it came, was no simple consequence of a series of individual and mistaken military decisions: it was implicit in the Nazi programme of military expansion and the racial state from the very start. Germany simply did not possess the resources of geopolitical supremacy (a point that became even clearer after the entry of the United States into the war in December 1941).

Surrounded by ruins, increasingly volatile in his moods and determined that no part of *his* Germany should outlive him (he had ordered a scorched earth policy in the face of the Allied advances), Hitler committed suicide in the bunker of the Reich Chancellery in Berlin on 30 April 1945. Within a few days the Third Reich capitulated and ceased to exist.

Conclusion

It is dangerous to see in the collapse of the Weimar Republic and the rise of Hitler some kind of German peculiarity. Democracies collapsed all over Europe between the wars (and indeed many have done so since). Furthermore, fascist movements enjoyed relatively strong support not only in Italy and Germany but also in Rumania and Hungary; and such movements were to be found in most other European countries too. Furthermore Hitler's views were sadly far from unique; rather they mirrored those of many of his contemporaries in Central and Eastern Europe, where ethnic resentments smouldered. The strength of ethnic identity and hatred has been made only too clear again in some parts of Eastern Europe since 1989, especially in the former Yugoslavia and in parts of what was the Soviet Union. Yet Hitler's ability to mobilise popular support at the end of the Weimar Republic, although it failed to win a majority of electors before 1933, was not simply a consequence of a general European malaise. It was also a result of specifically German problems, and in particular the absence of a democratic consensus and the multiple difficulties faced by the new Republic (described in Chapter 2). Even in this case, however, the evidence suggests that voters were swayed less by irrational prejudices and more by their immediate material interests and difficulties. Indeed, many of Weimar's problems resembled those of other welfare states in economic crisis. The prominence of daily economic survival also explains, as I tried to show in Chapter 2, why the Republic collapsed when it did, that is, in the depression of

1929–33, and not during the earlier inflationary years, which were not an unmitigated disaster for many. The dynamic Nazi movement, populist and not identified with the system, was then able to collaborate with other right-wing groups to bring Hitler to power. Whether the older conservative politicians and army officers, or even the Nazi electorate itself had a clue as to what would actually follow Hitler's assumption of power is more than a little doubtful, especially as the former thought they would be able to control the Führer, while the voting behaviour of the latter had little to do with war or anti-semitism.

This last point, of course, raises an important moral and historical question: namely, how could the people of a supposedly civilised country become implicated in the horrific barbarism of the Nazi state, which murdered not only its political enemies but whole categories of 'misfits' and 'outsiders', including gypsies and Jews? Part of the answer lies in the terroristic nature of the Third Reich, described in Chapter 3, part in privatisation and the retreat of individuals from the public arena, engendered by the destruction of mechanisms of public protest and collective solidarity. Yet, most chilling of all, much of what the Nazis did rested upon relatively common and mundane prejudices (what Detlev Peukert chooses to call the 'pathology of the modern'): a dislike of 'outsiders', of people who don't fit, such as tramps, gypsies, homosexuals, communists. It also rested upon the willingness of some Germans to denounce their neighbours, though such denunciations were rarely motivated by ideological conviction. Thus, although it never succeeded in brainwashing an entire people, the Nazi regime was able to rely on the support of many Germans as far as a good number of its policies were concerned, especially where these played on the strings of long-held beliefs and attitudes, as in the cases of nationalism, anti-socialism and traditional family values. Some individuals, against all the odds and at risk of life and limb, did resist. Indeed, far more did so than is normally imagined. It is to them that this small volume is dedicated.

Select bibliography

Abel, T. (1966) *The Nazi Movement* (New York).

Abraham, D. (1986) *The Collapse of the Weimar Republic*, 2nd edn (New York).

Abrams, L. and Harvey, E. (1996) *Gender Relations in German History* (London).

Allen, W.S. (1966) *The Nazi Seizure of Power* (London).

Aly, G. *et al.* (1994) *Cleansing the Fatherland* (Baltimore).

Aly, G. (1999) *The Final Solution* (London).

Arendt, H. (1958) *The Origins of Totalitarianism* (London).

Aycoberry, P. (1981) *The Nazi Question* (London).

Baird, J.W. (1975) *The Mythical World of Nazi Propaganda* (Oxford).

Balderston, T. (1993) *The Origins and Course of the German Economic Crisis* (Berlin).

Baldwin, P. (ed.) (1990) *Reworking the Past: Hitler, the Holocaust and the Historians* (Boston).

Bankier, D. (1992) *The Germans and the Final Solution* (Oxford).

Baranowski, S. (1995) *The Sanctity of Rural Life* (New Haven).

Barkai, A. (1990) *Nazi Economics* (Oxford).

Barnett, V. (1992) *For the Soul of the People* (London).

Bartov, O. (1988) *The Eastern Front* (London).

—— (1991) *Hitler's Army* (Oxford).

—— (1996) *Murder in our Midst* (New York).

Bauer, Y. (1978) *The Holocaust in Historical Perspective* (London).

Bauer, Z. (1992) *The Holocaust and Modernity* (New York).

Baynes, N.H. (ed.) (1942) *The Speeches of Adolf Hitler* (Oxford).

Beetham, D. (1983) *Marxists in the Face of Fascism* (Manchester).

Berg, D.R. (1983) *The Old Prussian Church and the Weimar Republic* (London).

Berger, D. L. (1996) *Twisted Cross. The German Christian Movement* (Chapel Hill, N.C.).

Bessel, R. (1981) *Political Violence and the Rise of Nazism* (London).

—— (ed.) (1987) *Daily Life in the Third Reich* (Oxford).

—— (1993) *Germany after the First World War* (Cambridge).

—— (ed.) (1996) *Fascist Italy and Nazi Germany* (Cambridge).

—— and E.J. Feuchtwanger (eds) (1981) *Social Change and Political Development in the Weimar Republic* (London).

Beyerchen, A.D. (1977) *Scientists under Hitler* (New Haven).

Binion, R. (1976) *Hitler among the Germans* (Oxford).

Bock, G. and Thane, P. (1990) *Maternity and Gender Politics* (London).

Bookbinder, P. (1996) *Weimar Germany* (London).

Bracher, K.D. (1973) *The German Dictatorship* (London).

Bramsted, E.K. (1965) *Goebbels and National Socialist Propaganda* (Michigan).

Breitmann, R. (1991) *The Architect of Genocide: Heinrich Himmler* (New York).

Bridenthal, R. *et al.* (eds) (1984) *When Biology Became Destiny* (New York).

—— and Koonz, C. (eds) (1977) *Becoming Visible* (London).

Broszat, M. (1981) *The Hitler State* (London).

—— (1987a) *Hitler and the Collapse of Weimar Germany* (Leamington Spa).

—— (1987b) 'Hitler and the genesis of the Final Solution', in H.W. Koch (ed.) *Aspects of the Third Reich* (London).

Browder, C. (1997) *Hitler's Enforcers* (Oxford).

Browning, C.R. (1978) *The Final Solution and the German Foreign Office* (New York).

—— (1987) *Fateful Months* (New York).

—— (ed.) (1992) *The Path to Genocide* (Cambridge).

—— (1992) *Ordinary Men* (London).

Brustein, W. (1998) *The Logic of Evil* (New Haven).

Buchheim, H., Broszat, M., Jacobson, H.A. and Krausnick, H. (1968) *Anatomy of the SS State* (London).

Bullock, A. (1952) *Hitler* (London).

—— (1991) *Parallel Lives. Hitler and Stalin* (London).

Burleigh, M. and Wipperman, W. (1993) *The Racial State* (Cambridge).

—— (1994) *Death and Deliverance. 'Euthanasia in Germany'* (Cambridge).

—— (1999) *Ethics and Extermination* (Cambridge).

—— (eds) (1996) *Confronting the Nazi Past* (London).

Burrin, P. (1994) *Hitler and the Jews* (London).

Caplan, J. (1988) *Government without Administration* (Oxford).

Carr, W. (1979) *Arms, Autarky and Aggression*, 2nd edn (London).

—— (1986) *Hitler. A Study in Personality and Politics*, 2nd edn (London).

Carroll, B. (1963) *Total War* (The Hague).

Carsten, F.L. (1966) *The Reichswehr and Politics* (Oxford).

—— (1967) *The Rise of Fascism* (London).

Cecil, R. (1972) *The Myth of the Master Race* (London).

Cesarini, D. (ed.) (1994) *The Final Solution* (London).

Childers, T. (1983) *The Nazi Voter* (Chapel Hill, N.C.).

—— (ed.) (1986) *The Formation of the Nazi Constituency* (London).

—— and Kaplan, J. (1993) *Reevaluating the Third Reich* (New York).

Cohn, N. (1970) *Warrant for Genocide* (London).

Conway, J. (1978) *The Nazi Persecution of the Churches* (London).

Cooper, M. (1978) *The German Army, 1933–45* (London).

Corni, G. (1990) *Hitler and the Peasants* (Oxford).

Crew, D. (ed.) (1994) *Nazism and German Society* (London).

Crew, D. (1998) *Germans on Welfare* (Oxford).

Dahrendorf, R. (1966) *Society and Democracy in Germany* (London).

Davidson, E. (1977) *The Making of Hitler* (London).

Dawidowicz, L.S. (1975) *The War against the Jews* (New York).

Deist, W. (1981) *The Wehrmacht and German Rearmament* (London).

Deutscher, H.C. (1974) *Hitler and his Germans* (Minnesota).

Diehl, J.M. (1977) *Paramilitary Politics in the Weimar Republic* (Bloomington).

Dorpalen, A. (1974) *Hindenburg and the Weimar Republic* (London).

Dullfer, J. (1996) *Nazi Germany* (London).

Eley, G. (1983) 'What produces Fascism?', in *Politics and Society* 12, pp. 57–82.

—— (1986) *From Unification to Nazism* (London).

Erikson, R.P. (1977) 'Theologians in the Third Reich', in *Journal of Contemporary History*, 12, pp. 595–615.

Eschenburg, T. (ed.) (1970) *The Road to Dictatorship* (London).

Evans, R.J. (1989) *In Hitler's Shadow* (London).

—— and D. Geary (1987) *The German Unemployed* (London).

Farquharson, J.G. (1976) *The Plough and the Swastika* (London).

Fest, J. (1972) *The Face of the Third Reich* (London).

—— (1974) *Hitler* (London).

—— (1996) *Plotting Hitler's Death* (London).

Fischer, C. (1983) *Stormtroopers* (London).

—— (1995) *The Rise of the Nazis* (Manchester).

—— (1996) *Weimar, the Working Classes and the Rise of National Socialism* (Oxford).

Fischer, K.P. (1995) *Nazi Germany* (London).

Fleming, G. (1986) *Hitler and the Final Solution* (Oxford).

Fox, J.P. (1979) 'Adolf Hitler. The debate continues', in *International Affairs* 55, pp. 252–65.

Frei, N. (1993) *National Socialist Rule in Germany* (Oxford).

Friedlander, H. (1995) *The Origins of Nazi Genocide* (Chapel Hill, N.C.).

Friedländer, S. (1992) *Probing the Limits of Representation* (Cambridge, Mass.).

—— (1998) *Nazi Germany and the Jews*, vol. 1, *The Years of Persecution* (London).

Fritzsche, P. (1990) *Germans into Nazis* (New York).

Geary, D. (1983a) 'The failure of German labour in the Weimar Republic', in M. Dobkowski and I. Wallimann (eds), *Towards the Holocaust* (Westport, Conn.), pp. 177–96.

—— (1983b) 'The industrial elite and the Nazis', in P.D. Stachura (ed.) *The Nazi Machtergreifung* (London), pp. 85–100.

—— (1985) 'Nazis and workers', in *European Studies Review*, xv (4), pp. 453–64.

—— (1990) 'Employers, workers and the collapse of the Weimar Republic', in I. Kershaw (ed.) *Weimar: The Failure of German Democracy* (London), pp. 92–119.

Gellately, R. (1990) *The Gestapo and German Society* (Oxford).

Giles, G.J. (1985) *Students and National Socialism* (Princeton).

Gillingham, J.R. (1985) *Industry and Politics in the Third Reich* (London).

Goldhagen, D.J. (1996) *Hitler's Willing Executioners* (New York).

Gordon, H.J. (1957) *The Reichswehr and the German Republic* (Princeton).

—— (1972) *Hitler and the Beer Hall Putsch* (Princeton).

Gordon, S. (1984) *Hitler, Germans and the 'Jewish Question'* (Princeton).

Gregor, N. (1998) *Daimler-Benz in the Third Reich* (New Haven).

Griffin, R. (ed.) (1998) *International Fascism* (London).

Grill, J.P.H. (1983) *The Nazi Party in Baden* (Chapel Hill).

Grunberger, R. (1971) *Social History of the Third Reich* (London).

Haffner, S. (1979) *The Meaning of Hitler* (London).

Hale, O.J. (1964) *The Captive Press in the Third Reich* (Princeton).

Hamilton, P.H. (1982) *Who Voted for Hitler?* (Princeton).

Harvey, E. (1993) *Youth and the Welfare State in Weimar Germany* (Oxford).

Hayes, P. (1987) *Industry and Ideology* (Cambridge).

Heberle, R. (1970) *From Democracy to Nazism* (New York).

Heiber, H. (1973) *Goebbels* (London).

Helmrich, E.C. (1979) *The German Churches under Hitler* (Detroit).

Herbert, U. (1997) *Hitler's Foreign Workers* (Cambridge).

Hiden, J. (1996) *Republican and Fascist Germany* (London).

—— and Farquharson, J. (1983) *Explaining Hitler's Germany* (London).

Hilberg, R. (1960) *The Destruction of the European Jews* (Chicago).

—— (1992) *Perpetrators, Victims, Bystanders* (New York).

Hildebrand, K. (1968) *The Third Reich* (London).

—— (1973) *The Foreign Policy of the Third Reich* (London).

Hirschfeld, G. (ed.) (1986) *The Politics of Genocide* (London).

—— and Kettenacker, L. (eds) (1981) *The Führer State* (Stuttgart).

Hitler, A. (1953) *Table Talk* (London).

—— (1960) *Mein Kampf*, ed. D.C. Watt (London).

Hoffmann, H. (1996) *The Triumph of Propaganda* (Oxford).

Hoffmann, P. (1974) *The German Resistance* (London).

—— (1997) *History of the German Resistance* (London).

Höhne, H. (1972) *The Order of the Death's Head* (London).

Holborn, H. (ed.) (1981) *Republic to Reich* (Stuttgart).

Hood, C.B. (1989) *Hitler. The Path to Power* (London).

Housden, M. (1996) *Resistance and Conformity in the Third Reich* (London).

Hunt, R.N. (1966) *German Social Democracy, 1918–1933* (Princeton).

Irving, D. (1977) *Hitler's War* (London).

Jablowsky, D. (1989) *The Nazi Party in Dissolution* (London).

Jäckel, E. (1972) *Hitler's Weltanschauung* (Middleton, Conn.).

—— (1978) *Hitler in History* (London).

James, H. (1986) *The German Slump* (Oxford).

Jenks, W.A. (1960) *Vienna and the Young Hitler* (New York).

Jones, L.E. (1972) 'The dying middle', in *Central European History*, 5, pp. 23–54.

—— (1986) 'Crisis and realignment in the late Weimar Republic', in R. Moeller (ed.), *Peasants and Lords in Modern Germany* (London).

—— and Retallack, J. (1989) *Between Reform, Reaction and Resistance* (London).

—— and Retallack, J. (1993) *Elections, Mass Politics and Social Change in Germany* (London).

Kater, M. (1983) *The Nazi Party* (Oxford).

—— (1989) *Doctors under Hitler* (New York).

—— (1992) *Different Drummers. Jazz in the Third Reich* (New York).

—— (1998) *The Twisted Muse. Music in the Third Reich* (New York).

Kehe, H. and Langmaid, J. (1987) *The Nazi Era* (London).

Kele, M.H. (1972) *Nazis and Workers* (Chapel Hill).

Kershaw, I. (1983) *Popular Opinion and Public Dissent* (Oxford).

—— (1989a) *The 'Hitler Myth'* (Oxford).

—— (1989b) *The Nazi Dictatorship*, 2nd edn (London).

—— (1991) *Hitler. Profile in Power* (London).

—— (1999) *Hitler*, vol. 1, *Hubris, 1889–1937* (London).

—— (2000) *Hitler*, vol. 2, *Nemesis, 1938–45* (London).

—— (ed.) (1990) *Weimar: The Failure of German Democracy* (London).

—— and Lewin, M. (1997) *Stalinism and Nazism* (London).

Kitchen, M. (1970) *Fascism* (London).

Klemperer, K. von (1992) *The German Resistance against Hitler* (London).

Koch, H.W. (1975) *The Hitler Youth* (London).

—— (ed.) (1987) *Aspects of the Third Reich* (London).

Kolb, E. (1986) *The Weimar Republic* (London).

Koonz, C. (1987) *Mothers in the Fatherland* (London).

Koshar, R. (1986) *Social Life, Politics and Nazism* (Chapel Hill).

Kruedener, R. von (ed.) (1990) *Economic Crisis and Political Collapse in the Weimar Republic* (Oxford).

Kuehl, S. (1994) *The Nazi Connection: Eugenics, American Racism and National Socialism* (Princeton).

Laffan, M. (ed.) (1988) *The Burden of German History* (London).

Landau, R. (1992) *The Nazi Holocaust* (London).

Langer, W. (1972) *The Mind of Adolf Hitler* (New York).

Laqueur, W. (1979) *Fascism*, 2nd edn (London).

Larsen, U. *et al.* (1980) *Who were the Fascists?* (Bergen).

Lebovics, H. (1969) *Social Conservatism and the Middle Class in Germany* (Princeton).

Leopold, J.A. (1977) *Alfred Hugenberg* (New Haven, Conn.).

Levi, E. (1994) *Music in the Third Reich* (New York).

Levy, R. S. (1975) *The Downfall of the Anti-Semitic Political Parties in Imperial Germany* (New Haven).

Maier, C.S. (1988) *The Unmasterable Past* (Cambridge, Mass.).

Marrus, M. (1987) 'The history of the Holocaust', in *Journal of Modern History*, 59, pp. 114ff.

—— (1987) *The Holocaust in History* (Hanover, N.H.).

Maser, W. (1970) *Hitler's* Mein Kampf (London).

—— (1973) *Hitler* (London).

Mason, A.W. (1966) 'Labour in the Third Reich', in *Past and Present* 33, pp. 112ff.

—— (1977) 'National Socialism and the German working class 1925–33', in *New German Critique*, 1, pp. 2–32.

—— (1981) 'Intention and explanation: a current controversy about the interpretation of National Socialism', in G. Hirschfeld and L. Kettenacker (eds), *The Führer State* (Stuttgart) pp. 23–42.

—— (1992) *Social Policy in the Third Reich* (Oxford).

—— (1993) *Fascism, Nazism and the Working Classes* (Oxford).

Mayer, A. J. (1988) *Why did the Heavens not Darken?* (New York).

Meding, D. von (1997) *Courageous Hearts* (Oxford).

Merkl, J.P. (1975) *Political Violence under the Swastika* (Princeton).

—— (1980) *The Making of a Stormtrooper* (Princeton).

Merson, A. (1985) *Communist Resistance in Nazi Germany* (London).

Milward, A. (1965) *The German Economy at War* (London).

Mommsen, H. (1979) 'National Socialism: continuity and change', in W. Laqueur, *Fascism*, 2nd edn (London) pp. 43–72.

—— (1986) 'The realisation of the unthinkable', in G. Hirschfeld (ed.) *The Policies of Genocide* (London).

—— (1991) *From Weimar to Auschwitz* (Oxford).

—— (1998) *The Rise and Fall of Weimar Germany* (Chapel Hill, N.C.).

Mosse, G.L. (1966a) *Nazi Culture* (London).

—— (1966b) *The Crisis of German Ideology* (London).

—— (1975) *The Nationalisation of the Masses* (New York).

—— (1979) *Nazism* (Oxford).

Mühlberger, D. (1980) 'The sociology of the NSDAP', in *Journal of Contemporary History*, 15, pp. 493ff.

—— (ed.) (1987) *The Social Bases of European Fascism* (London).

—— (1991) *Hitler's Followers* (London).

Müller, K.-J. (1984) *Army, Politics and Society in Germany, 1933–1945* (Manchester).

Müller-Hill, B. (1998) *Murderous Science* (Oxford).

Neumann, F. (1944) *Behemoth* (Oxford).

Nicholls, A. (1989) *Weimar and the Rise of Hitler,* 2nd edn (London).

—— and E. Matthias (1971) *German Democracy and the Triumph of Hitler* (London).

Niewyk, D.L. (1980) *The Jews in Weimar Germany* (London).

—— (1992) *The Holocaust* (Lexington).

Noakes, J. (1971) *The Nazi Party in Lower Saxony* (Oxford).

—— (1983) 'Nazism and revolution', in N. O'Sullivan (ed.), *Revolutionary Theory and Political Reality* (London) pp. 73–93.

—— (1984) 'Nazism and Eugenics' in Bullen, R. J. *et al., Ideas into Politics* (London).

—— (1990) *Government, Party and People in Nazi Germany* (Exeter).

—— and G. Pridham (1983–97) *Nazism, A Documentary Reader,* 4 vols (Exeter).

Nolte, E. (1964) *Three Faces of Fascism* (New York).

O'Neill, R.J. (1966) *The German Army and the Nazi Party* (London).

Orlow, D. (1971–3) *History of the Nazi Party,* 2 vols (London).

Overy, R. (1982) *The Nazi Economic Recovery* (London).

—— (1984) *Goering. The 'Iron Man'* (London).

—— (1994) *War and Economy in the Third Reich* (Oxford).

Owings, A. (1995) *Frauen* (London).

Peterson, E.N. (1969) *The Limits of Hitler's Power* (Princeton).

Peukert, D. (1987) *Inside Nazi Germany* (London).

—— (1991) *The Weimar Republic* (London).

Picker, H. (1974) *The Hitler Phenomenon* (London).

Pine, L. (1997) *Nazi Family Policy* (Oxford).

Poulantzas, N. (1974) *Fascism and Dictatorship* (London).

Pridham, G. (1983) *Hitler's Rise to Power* (London).

Proctor, R.N. (1988) *Racial Hygiene* (Cambridge, Mass.).

Pulzer, D.G. (1964) *The Rise of Political Anti-Semitism in Germany and Austria* (New York).

Rauschning, H. (1989) *Hitler Speaks* (London).

Reitlinger, G. (1968) *The Final Solution* (London).

Rempel, G. (1998) *Hitler's Children* (Chapel Hill)

Renneberg, M. and Walter, M. (eds) (1994) *Science, Technology and National Socialism* (Cambridge).

Rindoh, W. and Norling, B. (1995) *The Nazi Impact on a German Village* (Lexington).

Rosenhaft, E. (1983) *Beating the Fascists?* (Cambridge).

Saunders, T. (1992) 'The Nazis and Social Revolution' in Martel, G. (ed.) *Modern Germany Reconsidered* (London).

95

Sax, B. and Kuntz, D. (1992) *Inside Hitler's Germany* (Lexington).

Schleunes, K.A. (1970) *The Twisted Road to Auschwitz* (London).

Schmidt, M. (1984) *Albert Speer* (New York).

Schmidt, U. (1999) *Medical Research Films, Perpetrators and Victims in National Socialist Germany* (Husum).

Schoenbaum, D. (1966) *Hitler's Social Revolution* (London).

Schramm, P.E. (1972) *Hitler. The Man and Military Leader* (London).

Schweitzer, A. (1964) *Big Business in the Third Reich* (London).

Shirer, W. (1961) *The Rise and Fall of the Third Reich* (New York).

Silverman, D.P. (1998) *Hitler's Economy* (London).

Smelser, R. (1988) *Robert Ley* (Oxford).

Smith, B.F. (1967) *Adolf Hitler. His Family, Childhood and Youth* (Stanford).

Smith, W.B. (1989) *The Ideological Origins of Nazi Imperialism* (London).

Sohn-Rethel, A. (1970) *Economic and Class Structure of German Fascism* (London).

Speer, A. (1970) *Inside the Third Reich* (London).

Speier, H. (1986) *German White Collar Workers and the Rise of Hitler* (New Haven, Conn.).

Stachura, P.D. (1975) *Nazi Youth and the Weimar Republic* (Santa Barbara).

—— (1983) *Gregor Strasser* (London).

—— (1986) *Unemployment and the Great Depression in Weimar Germany* (London).

—— (ed.) (1978) *The Shaping of the Nazi State* (London).

—— (1983) *The Nazi Machtergreifung* (London).

—— (1989) *The Weimar Republic and the Younger Proletariat* (London).

Steinberg, J. (1990) *All or Nothing: The Axis and the Holocaust* (London).

Steinberg, M.S. (1977) *Brownshirts* (Chicago).

Stephenson, J. (1976) *Women in Nazi Society* (London).

—— (1981) *The Nazi Organization of Women* (London).

Stern, F.R. (1961) *The Politics of Cultural Despair* (Berkeley).

Stern, J.P. (1974) *Hitler* (London).

Stierlein, H. (1978) *Adolf Hitler. A Family Perspective* (New York).

Stoakes, G. (1987) *Hitler and the Quest for World Dominion* (Leamington Spa).

Stone, N. (1980) *Hitler* (London).

Strawson, J. (1971) *Hitler as a Military Commander* (London).

Szejnmann, C.-C. (1998) *Nazism in Central Germany* (Oxford).

Toland, J. (1976) *Adolf Hitler* (New York).

Trevor-Roper, H.R. (1947) *The Last Days of Hitler* (London).

Turner, H.A. (1985) *Big Business and the Rise of Hitler* (Oxford).

—— (ed.) (1972) *Nazism and the Third Reich* (New York).

Unger, A.H. (1974) *The Totalitarian Party* (Cambridge).

Waite, R.G.C. (1977) *Hitler. The Psychopathic God* (New York).

Weinberg, G, (1995) *Germany, Hitler and World War II* (Cambridge).

Weindling, P. (1989) *Health, Race and German Politics* (Cambridge).

Welch, D. (1983) *Propaganda and the German Cinema* (London).

—— (ed.) (1988) *Nazi Propaganda* (London).

—— (1993) *The Third Reich* (London).

—— (1998) *Hitler* (London).

Wheeler-Bennett, J.W. (1953) *The Nemesis of Power* (London).

Woolf, S. (1968a) *European Fascism* (London).

—— (ed.) (1968b) *The Nature of Fascism* (London).

Zeman, Z.A.B. (1964) *Nazi Propaganda* (Oxford).

Zentner, C. and Beduerfnis, F. (1997) *The Encyclopedia of the Third Reich* (Da Capo, Penn.).